FREE Test Taking Tips DVD Offer

To help us better serve you, we have developed a Test Taking Tips DVD that we would like to give you for FREE. **This DVD covers world-class test taking tips that you can use to be even more successful when you are taking your test.**

All that we ask is that you email us your feedback about your study guide. Please let us know what you thought about it – whether that is good, bad or indifferent.

To get your **FREE Test Taking Tips DVD**, email freedvd@studyguideteam.com with "FREE DVD" in the subject line and the following information in the body of the email:

  a. The title of your study guide.

  b. Your product rating on a scale of 1-5, with 5 being the highest rating.

  c. Your feedback about the study guide. What did you think of it?

  d. Your full name and shipping address to send your free DVD.

If you have any questions or concerns, please don't hesitate to contact us at freedvd@studyguideteam.com.

Thanks again!

AP US Government and Politics 2019 & 2020 Prep Book

AP United States Government and Politics Study Guide & Practice Test Questions [Updated for the NEW Outline]

Test Prep Books

Table of Contents

Quick Overview

As you draw closer to taking your exam, effective preparation becomes more and more important. Thankfully, you have this study guide to help you get ready. Use this guide to help keep your studying on track and refer to it often.

This study guide contains several key sections that will help you be successful on your exam. The guide contains tips for what you should do the night before and the day of the test. Also included are test-taking tips. Knowing the right information is not always enough. Many well-prepared test takers struggle with exams. These tips will help equip you to accurately read, assess, and answer test questions.

A large part of the guide is devoted to showing you what content to expect on the exam and to helping you better understand that content. In this guide are practice test questions so that you can see how well you have grasped the content. Then, answer explanations are provided so that you can understand why you missed certain questions.

Don't try to cram the night before you take your exam. This is not a wise strategy for a few reasons. First, your retention of the information will be low. Your time would be better used by reviewing information you already know rather than trying to learn a lot of new information. Second, you will likely become stressed as you try to gain a large amount of knowledge in a short amount of time. Third, you will be depriving yourself of sleep. So be sure to go to bed at a reasonable time the night before. Being well-rested helps you focus and remain calm.

Be sure to eat a substantial breakfast the morning of the exam. If you are taking the exam in the afternoon, be sure to have a good lunch as well. Being hungry is distracting and can make it difficult to focus. You have hopefully spent lots of time preparing for the exam. Don't let an empty stomach get in the way of success!

When travelling to the testing center, leave earlier than needed. That way, you have a buffer in case you experience any delays. This will help you remain calm and will keep you from missing your appointment time at the testing center.

Be sure to pace yourself during the exam. Don't try to rush through the exam. There is no need to risk performing poorly on the exam just so you can leave the testing center early. Allow yourself to use all of the allotted time if needed.

Remain positive while taking the exam even if you feel like you are performing poorly. Thinking about the content you should have mastered will not help you perform better on the exam.

Once the exam is complete, take some time to relax. Even if you feel that you need to take the exam again, you will be well served by some down time before you begin studying again. It's often easier to convince yourself to study if you know that it will come with a reward!

Test-Taking Strategies

1. Predicting the Answer

When you feel confident in your preparation for a multiple-choice test, try predicting the answer before reading the answer choices. This is especially useful on questions that test objective factual knowledge. By predicting the answer before reading the available choices, you eliminate the possibility that you will be distracted or led astray by an incorrect answer choice. You will feel more confident in your selection if you read the question, predict the answer, and then find your prediction among the answer choices. After using this strategy, be sure to still read all of the answer choices carefully and completely. If you feel unprepared, you should not attempt to predict the answers. This would be a waste of time and an opportunity for your mind to wander in the wrong direction.

2. Reading the Whole Question

Too often, test takers scan a multiple-choice question, recognize a few familiar words, and immediately jump to the answer choices. Test authors are aware of this common impatience, and they will sometimes prey upon it. For instance, a test author might subtly turn the question into a negative, or he or she might redirect the focus of the question right at the end. The only way to avoid falling into these traps is to read the entirety of the question carefully before reading the answer choices.

3. Looking for Wrong Answers

Long and complicated multiple-choice questions can be intimidating. One way to simplify a difficult multiple-choice question is to eliminate all of the answer choices that are clearly wrong. In most sets of answers, there will be at least one selection that can be dismissed right away. If the test is administered on paper, the test taker could draw a line through it to indicate that it may be ignored; otherwise, the test taker will have to perform this operation mentally or on scratch paper. In either case, once the obviously incorrect answers have been eliminated, the remaining choices may be considered. Sometimes identifying the clearly wrong answers will give the test taker some information about the correct answer. For instance, if one of the remaining answer choices is a direct opposite of one of the eliminated answer choices, it may well be the correct answer. The opposite of obviously wrong is obviously right! Of course, this is not always the case. Some answers are obviously incorrect simply because they are irrelevant to the question being asked. Still, identifying and eliminating some incorrect answer choices is a good way to simplify a multiple-choice question.

4. Don't Overanalyze

Anxious test takers often overanalyze questions. When you are nervous, your brain will often run wild, causing you to make associations and discover clues that don't actually exist. If you feel that this may be a problem for you, do whatever you can to slow down during the test. Try taking a deep breath or counting to ten. As you read and consider the question, restrict yourself to the particular words used by the author. Avoid thought tangents about what the author *really* meant, or what he or she was *trying* to say. The only things that matter on a multiple-choice test are the words that are actually in the question. You must avoid reading too much into a multiple-choice question, or supposing that the writer meant something other than what he or she wrote.

5. No Need for Panic

It is wise to learn as many strategies as possible before taking a multiple-choice test, but it is likely that you will come across a few questions for which you simply don't know the answer. In this situation, avoid panicking. Because most multiple-choice tests include dozens of questions, the relative value of a single wrong answer is small. As much as possible, you should compartmentalize each question on a multiple-choice test. In other words, you should not allow your feelings about one question to affect your success on the others. When you find a question that you either don't understand or don't know how to answer, just take a deep breath and do your best. Read the entire question slowly and carefully. Try rephrasing the question a couple of different ways. Then, read all of the answer choices carefully. After eliminating obviously wrong answers, make a selection and move on to the next question.

6. Confusing Answer Choices

When working on a difficult multiple-choice question, there may be a tendency to focus on the answer choices that are the easiest to understand. Many people, whether consciously or not, gravitate to the answer choices that require the least concentration, knowledge, and memory. This is a mistake. When you come across an answer choice that is confusing, you should give it extra attention. A question might be confusing because you do not know the subject matter to which it refers. If this is the case, don't eliminate the answer before you have affirmatively settled on another. When you come across an answer choice of this type, set it aside as you look at the remaining choices. If you can confidently assert that one of the other choices is correct, you can leave the confusing answer aside. Otherwise, you will need to take a moment to try to better understand the confusing answer choice. Rephrasing is one way to tease out the sense of a confusing answer choice.

7. Your First Instinct

Many people struggle with multiple-choice tests because they overthink the questions. If you have studied sufficiently for the test, you should be prepared to trust your first instinct once you have carefully and completely read the question and all of the answer choices. There is a great deal of research suggesting that the mind can come to the correct conclusion very quickly once it has obtained all of the relevant information. At times, it may seem to you as if your intuition is working faster even than your reasoning mind. This may in fact be true. The knowledge you obtain while studying may be retrieved from your subconscious before you have a chance to work out the associations that support it. Verify your instinct by working out the reasons that it should be trusted.

8. Key Words

Many test takers struggle with multiple-choice questions because they have poor reading comprehension skills. Quickly reading and understanding a multiple-choice question requires a mixture of skill and experience. To help with this, try jotting down a few key words and phrases on a piece of scrap paper. Doing this concentrates the process of reading and forces the mind to weigh the relative importance of the question's parts. In selecting words and phrases to write down, the test taker thinks about the question more deeply and carefully. This is especially true for multiple-choice questions that are preceded by a long prompt.

9. Subtle Negatives

One of the oldest tricks in the multiple-choice test writer's book is to subtly reverse the meaning of a question with a word like *not* or *except*. If you are not paying attention to each word in the question, you can easily be led astray by this trick. For instance, a common question format is, "Which of the following is...?" Obviously, if the question instead is, "Which of the following is not...?," then the answer will be quite different. Even worse, the test makers are aware of the potential for this mistake and will include one answer choice that would be correct if the question were not negated or reversed. A test taker who misses the reversal will find what he or she believes to be a correct answer and will be so confident that he or she will fail to reread the question and discover the original error. The only way to avoid this is to practice a wide variety of multiple-choice questions and to pay close attention to each and every word.

10. Reading Every Answer Choice

It may seem obvious, but you should always read every one of the answer choices! Too many test takers fall into the habit of scanning the question and assuming that they understand the question because they recognize a few key words. From there, they pick the first answer choice that answers the question they believe they have read. Test takers who read all of the answer choices might discover that one of the latter answer choices is actually *more* correct. Moreover, reading all of the answer choices can remind you of facts related to the question that can help you arrive at the correct answer. Sometimes, a misstatement or incorrect detail in one of the latter answer choices will trigger your memory of the subject and will enable you to find the right answer. Failing to read all of the answer choices is like not reading all of the items on a restaurant menu: you might miss out on the perfect choice.

11. Spot the Hedges

One of the keys to success on multiple-choice tests is paying close attention to every word. This is never truer than with words like almost, most, some, and sometimes. These words are called "hedges" because they indicate that a statement is not totally true or not true in every place and time. An absolute statement will contain no hedges, but in many subjects, the answers are not always straightforward or absolute. There are always exceptions to the rules in these subjects. For this reason, you should favor those multiple-choice questions that contain hedging language. The presence of qualifying words indicates that the author is taking special care with his or her words, which is certainly important when composing the right answer. After all, there are many ways to be wrong, but there is only one way to be right! For this reason, it is wise to avoid answers that are absolute when taking a multiple-choice test. An absolute answer is one that says things are either all one way or all another. They often include words like *every*, *always*, *best*, and *never*. If you are taking a multiple-choice test in a subject that doesn't lend itself to absolute answers, be on your guard if you see any of these words.

12. Long Answers

In many subject areas, the answers are not simple. As already mentioned, the right answer often requires hedges. Another common feature of the answers to a complex or subjective question are qualifying clauses, which are groups of words that subtly modify the meaning of the sentence. If the question or answer choice describes a rule to which there are exceptions or the subject matter is complicated, ambiguous, or confusing, the correct answer will require many words in order to be expressed clearly and accurately. In essence, you should not be deterred by answer choices that seem excessively long. Oftentimes, the author of the text will not be able to write the correct answer without offering some qualifications and modifications. Your job is to read the answer choices thoroughly and completely and to select the one that most accurately and precisely answers the question.

13. Restating to Understand

Sometimes, a question on a multiple-choice test is difficult not because of what it asks but because of how it is written. If this is the case, restate the question or answer choice in different words. This process serves a couple of important purposes. First, it forces you to concentrate on the core of the question. In order to rephrase the question accurately, you have to understand it well. Rephrasing the question will concentrate your mind on the key words and ideas. Second, it will present the information to your mind in a fresh way. This process may trigger your memory and render some useful scrap of information picked up while studying.

14. True Statements

Sometimes an answer choice will be true in itself, but it does not answer the question. This is one of the main reasons why it is essential to read the question carefully and completely before proceeding to the answer choices. Too often, test takers skip ahead to the answer choices and look for true statements. Having found one of these, they are content to select it without reference to the question above. Obviously, this provides an easy way for test makers to play tricks. The savvy test taker will always read the entire question before turning to the answer choices. Then, having settled on a correct answer choice, he or she will refer to the original question and ensure that the selected answer is relevant. The mistake of choosing a correct-but-irrelevant answer choice is especially common on questions related to specific pieces of objective knowledge. A prepared test taker will have a wealth of factual knowledge at his or her disposal, and should not be careless in its application.

15. No Patterns

One of the more dangerous ideas that circulates about multiple-choice tests is that the correct answers tend to fall into patterns. These erroneous ideas range from a belief that B and C are the most common right answers, to the idea that an unprepared test-taker should answer "A-B-A-C-A-D-A-B-A." It cannot be emphasized enough that pattern-seeking of this type is exactly the WRONG way to approach a multiple-choice test. To begin with, it is highly unlikely that the test maker will plot the correct answers according to some predetermined pattern. The questions are scrambled and delivered in a random order. Furthermore, even if the test maker was following a pattern in the assignation of correct answers, there is no reason why the test taker would know which pattern he or she was using. Any attempt to discern a pattern in the answer choices is a waste of time and a distraction from the real work of taking the test. A test taker would be much better served by extra preparation before the test than by reliance on a pattern in the answers.

FREE DVD OFFER

Don't forget that doing well on your exam includes both understanding the test content and understanding how to use what you know to do well on the test. We offer a completely FREE Test Taking Tips DVD that covers world class test taking tips that you can use to be even more successful when you are taking your test.

All that we ask is that you email us your feedback about your study guide. To get your **FREE Test Taking Tips DVD**, email freedvd@studyguideteam.com with "FREE DVD" in the subject line and the following information in the body of the email:

- The title of your study guide.
- Your product rating on a scale of 1-5, with 5 being the highest rating.
- Your feedback about the study guide. What did you think of it?
- Your full name and shipping address to send your free DVD.

Introduction

Function of the Test

The Advanced Placement (AP) U.S. Government and Politics Exam is part of the College Board's Advanced Placement Program, which affords high school students the opportunity to pursue college-level coursework while in high school. Like every other exam in this program, the U.S. Government and Politics exam is the culminating final exam for its respective course. Taking the course and scoring well on the exam demonstrates to prospective colleges that a high school student has attempted the hardest course level available to them, and can even earn the student college credit or advanced placement.

The AP U.S. Government and Politics exam requires students to demonstrate their knowledge and understanding of the U.S. political system's policies, processes, perspectives, and behaviors. Questions will also involve defining, explaining, comparing, and interpreting political concepts of this system, and making connections between historical and contemporary issues in the U.S. political system.

Test Administration

The AP U.S. Government and Politics exam is offered on a certain date in May each year, and mainly administered by schools that offer an AP U.S. Government and Politics course. However, students can make arrangements with a school to take an AP exam even if they did not take the course at that particular school. All AP exams cost the same amount of money, with an additional fee added for exams administered outside of the U.S. and Canada. Schools can also add fees to cover their costs of administering the exams if they wish, but most offer the exams at the standard base rate.

Accommodations for students with documented disabilities include time extensions, large-type exams, large-block answer sheets, Braille devices, question readers, response writers, and more. Students seeking accommodations should contact the Disabilities Office of College Board Services.

Students may take an AP exam every time it is offered (i.e., once a year). Scores from all attempts will be reported in the score report after each test.

Test Format

There are two sections to the exam, which lasts a total of 3 hours. Section I contains 55 multiple-choice questions, lasts 80 minutes, and counts for 50% of the exam score. Section II contains 4 free-response questions, lasts 100 minutes, and also counts for 50% of the exam score. Multiple-choice questions may be of a variety of types, including quantitative analysis, qualitative analysis, concept application, visual analysis, comparison, and others. There is typically one free-response questions of each of the following types: concept application (where students must explain a given political scenario), quantitative analysis (where students must analyze and draw conclusions from data, graphs, or charts), SCOTUS comparison (where students compare Supreme Court cases), and an argument essay (where students craft an argumentative essay using foundational documents).

Scoring

Answers to the multiple-choice questions are scored by a machine, and students receive a raw score of one point for each correct answer. Answers to the free-response questions are scored by thousands of expert, trained AP teachers and college professors; these questions are scored on a scale that varies between three and ten points, depending on the length and complexity of the question. The free-response scores are weighted and then added to the multiple-choice scores. This raw score is then scaled to a composite AP score, which ranges from 1 to 5, with 5 being the maximal score. While there is no set passing score, most colleges and universities require a score of at least 3 to place out of a class, and a 4 or 5 to earn college credit. The AP score interpretation guide, which gives meaning to the scores such that they signify how qualified a student is to receive advanced placement or college credit, assigns the following recommendations for the possible AP scores: a score of 1 is assigned "no recommendation," 2 is "possibly qualified," 3 is "qualified," 4 is "well qualified," and a student who earns a score of 5 is considered "extremely well qualified."

In 2018, 13.3% of test takers earned a 5, 13.3% earned a 4, 26.4% earned a 3, 24.4% earned a 2, and 25.5% earned a 1.

Unit 1: Foundations of American Democracy

Liberty and Order

The U.S. Government is Based on Ideals of a Limited Government

From its inception through its creation by the Founding Fathers, the new United States government laid its foundation on the idea of **limited government**. The function, power, and abilities of a limited government are restricted in scope to pre-defined limits; in the United States, the Constitution establishes the limits. The government is granted domain over certain areas, yet cannot intervene in the domain of civil liberties as established in the Constitution.

Natural Rights
Under the idea of limited government, many subsets follow, the first of which is **natural rights**. The English philosopher John Locke coined the idea of natural rights as pertaining to "life, liberty, and property." While not directly stating "natural rights," the Declaration of Independence does draw upon Locke's famous quote in its opening lines, stating all people have the right to "life, liberty, and the pursuit of happiness." The populace possesses these natural rights and the government should not impede them.

Popular Sovereignty
Another key piece of limited government is **popular sovereignty**. The term refers to the people's consent to be governed. This concept was particularly important to early Americans after the rule of the British, and simply stated that a government draws its power from the people only. Put concisely, if a government loses the faith of its people, it is no longer a recognized government.

Social Contract
Related to popular sovereignty is the theory of the **social contract**. This idea, drawn from the teachings of Thomas Hobbes, was an integral part in the creation of the government. This theory is parallel to popular sovereignty in that it places importance on the consent of the governed. The social contract expresses the basic expectations of the people for their government. The people give up certain rights and they consent to be governed in exchange for the government protection of their other rights. This again draws on the idea of the people choosing to have their government, instead of a government being forced upon them.

Republicanism
Chief among the principles within the limited government that early America was predicated on was the principle of **republicanism**. Republicanism is the philosophy of most of the Founding Fathers who framed the Constitution. It stresses the individual and makes clear that, above all, personal liberty is the sole concern of the government. Republicanism is underlined in the Constitution as granting "unalienable rights" to all and that those rights are guaranteed, regardless of the majority. This belief was largely crafted from a healthy fear of large government, such as the monarchy the colonies had been subjected to before the American Revolution. Most importantly, the Founders believed that representatives should always represent the interests of the people who elect them. Thomas Jefferson championed this idea as protection from a corrupt government: the "citizens [are] the safest protector of their own rights."

The Declaration of Independence and the U.S. Constitution

As animosity from the colonies festered to a breaking point toward British rule because of the increasing British taxation, the leaders from the differing regions began to talk among themselves. Finally, in June of 1776, leaders from the thirteen colonies convened in Philadelphia to debate the notion of leaving the British Empire.

As the Continental Congress debated, opinion moved toward a resolution for independence. The delegates selected a committee of representatives to draft a document for independence, including Thomas Jefferson, Benjamin Franklin, and John Adams. Together, they worked to construct the document that would be sent to the colonies for approval of declaring their independence from Britain. After a month of deliberation, Jefferson, inspired by the influences of John Locke and Francis Bacon, drafted the **Declaration of Independence**, the document that defined the American Revolution.

In the Declaration, Jefferson drew upon Lockean principles stating that all are granted "unalienable rights," including "life, liberty, and the pursuit of happiness." Listing crimes levied against King George, the Declaration focused upon the social contract in saying that a government that fails to protect those rights is one that must be overthrown. In place of British rule, the Declaration established a new government that would protect the sovereign rights of all of its citizens.

Following the war, the delegates met to put those ideals into practice. The Philadelphia Convention was convened in the summer of 1787 with the goal of drafting a new United States Constitution. It would replace the **Articles of Confederation**, the first attempt at a government by the new United States that failed to provide the federal government with ample power to respond to specific threatens within the country.

At this convention, George Washington presided over a debate that shaped the future of the American government. The delegates debated a variety of alternatives, with some favoring minor changes to the current system, and others favoring an entirely new system. Once delegates agreed on a new form of government, the attention turned to a debate on government power at the federal and state levels, and the split of voting power. The discussion then turned to a "grand committee" that debated the differing aspects of the proposed plans.

Among the government plans were proposals by New York's Alexander Hamilton and Virginia's James Madison. Hamilton argued that a central government must be strong in order to succeed. Madison proposed a full system, called the **Virginia Plan**, that would become the basis of the new **United States Constitution**. Madison's plan favored larger states, arguing that they should receive a higher voting bloc in the legislature. Rivaling this was the **New Jersey Plan**, which argued that there should be equal representation to protect the smaller states. Ultimately, the parties settled on a plan that would be nicknamed the **Connecticut Compromise**. This plan stated that there should be two houses of Congress: one that was representative of the population of each state, called the **House of Representatives**, and another that held equal representation from each state, called the **Senate**. This bicameral approach to the legislature won over a majority of the delegates, with the convention voting to promote it as the new Constitution later in that year.

Representative Democracies

The democracy put in place as the government model for the United States would be one of a new age. In its design, the populace would vote on officials to represent them at the national level, in the House of Representatives and the Senate, as well as participate in a national popular vote for the presidency. In theory, the people would place the power to vote in the hands of their representatives. This form of democratic republic takes many forms under the U.S. system.

Participatory Democracy

A **participatory democracy** is a democratic system that pushes for the full participation of the populace in the political system. It encourages the voting public to be responsible for all of the policy choices; however, it differs from a direct democracy in that it still places the power to legislate with the representatives. Simply put, the people vote with policies in mind and it is the representatives' job to implement the policies.

Pluralist Democracy

Another piece of the democratic system is the **pluralist democracy**. This is a system in which groups— rather than a specific group or party—come together to aid in governing and legislating. In this type of democracy, people come together within groups centered around support of basic policy ideas and then move to vote on that issue to get their policy implemented; people focus on policies they support rather than a particular party or message.

Elite Democracy

As the Framers debated the establishment of the type of democratic republic the United States would resemble, a popular version of what it should be was an **elite democracy**. This particular form of democracy, embraced by many of those writing the original Constitution, argued for a more selective participation model. In this system, only the intelligent and wealthy decide what is best for the overall public good. This type of democracy was seen as a safeguard against a public that might not be best equipped to make the decisions that would become national policy for all Americans.

Written Responses About the Role of Government

With such differing types of democracy proposed, the Second Constitutional Convention saw significant infighting among the delegates about which was preferable. Chief among the issues in front of the delegates was the role of the government itself, and whether a democracy even needed or warranted the type of strong central government that was being advocated following the failure of the Articles of Confederation.

Once the original draft of the Constitution was written, it began to show the real pillars upon which the U.S. federal government would be based. The federal government would be able to grow in power, with an increased ability to respond to national threats. The Constitution established the separation of the legislature, executive, and judiciary branches to limit and check the balance of powers. It also established parameters for the federal government and limited its scope to a list of immediate powers.

Brutus No. 1

As talks pushed forward into the summer and the movement to ratify the new Constitution was getting stronger, differing factions began to let their opinions play out in the public. Among them was Robert Yates of New York. Yates, an Anti-Federalist, wrote an essay titled **Brutus No. 1**, directed at the people of New York. In it, he openly worried about the size and scope of the federal government that the original draft of the Constitution laid out. He argued that a land so diverse and widely populated couldn't possibly be governed in an adequate way without some giveaways of basic rights.

Federalist No. 10

In response, supporters of the Constitution, including Alexander Hamilton and James Madison, wrote a series of essays titled the Federalist Papers to quell some threats to the ratification. Chiefly, Madison's

Federalist No. 10 responded to Brutus's concerns by arguing that a stronger central government would be better equipped to safeguard the rights of the minority, and that republicanism would guide the federal, as well as the state, governments.

Contemporary Models of Representative Democracies

When thinking of forms of democracy in the United States today, all three of the debated types are still alive in the current political world. Participatory democracy is the one most commonly considered to represent the United States; however, that's not entirely accurate. Representatives make the policy decisions once elected, and can break from the public, but there is still a definite push for the public to participate. There are many varieties of this, from town halls to public-backed initiatives that drive interest from the voting public without necessarily channeling through politicians first. Some states have **referendums**, which are policy decisions voted on directly by the public. In any case, there are still pieces of participatory democracy within the U.S. republic, as the public may effect change in a variety of ways.

Hints of pluralist democracy are also prevalent in today's society. While the U.S. system has historically been a two-party political system, that is not to say that there are not hints of pluralist democracy as well. Lobbying firms and interest groups are the most common examples of this, with pockets of people coming together to support a particular movement and trying to make changes through their responses. This can influence voting and participation, while not necessarily subscribing to a particular political movement or group in power.

The other form of democracy, the elite democracy, is the one that seems to have aged the worst over time within our system, and yet, there is a good example of this system still in practice today in the United States: the **Electoral College**, which places a small group of delegates as a check against the popular vote of the presidency, if needed. This system allows people within the Electoral College a final vote after the popular vote for the presidency, to break from their state and vote for a differing candidate altogether if they feel that it is for the public good.

Constitutionalism

Federalist No. 10

Madison, along with Alexander Hamilton, wrote a significant portion of a packet of legal writings submitted to local papers, known as the **Federalist Papers**, to defend the new United States Constitution. As a wave of Anti-Federalist sentiment began to grow prior to the official signing of the Constitution, articles began popping up in newspapers rivaling the work of Madison and Hamilton.

Of the arguments made by the Anti-Federalists, chief was the one against a strong central republic. Anti-Federalists argued that a strong republic would make democracy hard for the minority and fail to address the needs of a large nation. Madison sought to answer those concerns with Federalist No. 10, an essay supporting a strong federal government.

Madison's argument in Federalist No. 10 addressed several concerns. The first, he argued, was that a strong central republic would be better at preventing the minority from being squashed by the majority. Madison argued that by having representation within both the House and the Senate, the minority would always have protectors, and the elected representatives would be inclined to represent both the minority and majority in their region.

Also, Madison argued that a republic would more evenly distribute power in a large country. With more representatives, the power between local, state, and federal governments would be more dispersed, and it would more easily control "the mischiefs of factions" that might overrun a democracy.

Most importantly, Madison argued that a large republic would do a better job of weeding out corrupt leaders. Madison reasoned that in a larger system with more opinions and people, it would be harder for politicians to abuse the system and run a game that could take advantage of their people and the political system; the large system would weed out those who would harm the republic as a whole.

Brutus No. 1

While it may seem like the adoption of the Constitution was a clear-cut decision, there was much worry within the states about this new form of government. However, there were other authors who had made it their mission to persuade the country that this new form of government was a dangerous threat to their newfound freedoms. George Clinton, Samuel Bryan, and Robert Yates are the most well-known of these writers.

Of the Anti-Federalists arguing against the Federalist authors Madison, Hamilton and John Jay, the most succinct of the arguments came from Brutus No. 1, a paper named for Brutus, the Roman senator who famously assassinated Julius Caesar to protect the Republic.

In Brutus, he made the case that the strong federal government proposed as the answer to the Articles of Confederation was much too large to be successful. On one hand, Brutus said that a large federal government would make the states almost useless in scope. With the powers of the republic, the states would have power within their borders only, and anything the federal government decided to push up them, they would have no choice but to accept. He argued that the Constitution guaranteed that the states would always be subservient to the federal republic.

Beyond this, Brutus also made the case that such a large land as the United States couldn't possibly be governed by one central republic. For starters, the sheer scope of the land mass would make governing and representing effectively almost impossible. Also, the plurality of opinions of the massive number of people in the United States would make the government not function at all, with too many opinions and points of view for the government to work efficiently.

The heaviest of Brutus's concerns was that he worried that a government like the one proposed would be so large that it would ignore its own voters, with representatives presiding over such large districts becoming completely detached from their voters at home and working in their own self-interest. Simply put, Brutus argued that the large republic would govern itself over the people and not represent anyone but its own interests.

Weaknesses of the Articles of Confederation

Despite the debates over the Constitution throughout that summer, few didn't see the need for a revamp of the system, at least in part, following the time under the **Articles of Confederation**. The first true laws of the new republic, the Articles of Confederation established the United States as exactly that: a confederation of states that operated almost as individual governments. States within the Union worked within their own borders, rarely coming together for anything aside from trading and distribution of different products.

As time wore on with this system, problems emerged throughout the nation. Once the Revolutionary War came to an end, the United States found itself in an unusual spot. States were sovereign and operating on their own within the Articles of Confederation, but there were the complications that come with a post-war period to deal with. The United States still owed money to foreign governments and many merchants within the States owed money to foreign merchants who aided them throughout the war. Because it was a young government, foreign countries and people didn't want to accept the new currency of the United States, preferring gold. So, as poor farmers and merchants tried to pay their debts, they were forced into paying with gold and other hard currencies that were difficult to obtain, without help from the government.

This came to a head in 1787, when Daniel Shay led a rebellion that seized the courthouses in Western Massachusetts. With them shut down, debts could not be collected, but the state of Massachusetts was unable to respond, and the federal government had no sitting army. Shay's Rebellion lasted months before a militia financed by local merchants was able to quash it before participants stormed a local Massachusetts armory.

This embarrassing display highlighted the massive shortcomings of the Articles of Confederation. On one hand, without a strong central government, problems like these could drag on interminably. It was only a matter of time before a more concerted effort caused more harm to the country. It also highlighted the country's ineffectiveness at 1) collecting taxes, and 2) the individual states working as one. Without unity, there was no negotiating with foreign powers or debtors, or the ability to pay for a sitting army, or pretty much anything else. As the threat of a greater rebellion throughout the nation grew, the Constitutional Convention convened the next year.

Necessary Compromises to Adopt and Ratify the Constitution

Once the convention convened, the delegates were faced with some difficult choices. The new U.S. Constitution needed some work and compromise, and many from each state had differing opinions on how the new federal government should work, as well as how it should integrate with state governments. In particular, larger states argued for representation by population, as the states that harbor the most people shouldn't have to abide by smaller state concerns. The smaller states disagreed, arguing that equal representation was necessary to make sure they weren't trampled over by the larger states.

The Connecticut Compromise
As the debate between the systems rambled on over the summer, eventually a middle ground was brokered between the two sides with the **Connecticut Compromise**. The proposal, combining elements from both sides, introduced a bicameral (two house) system for Congress. There would be the **Senate**, where each state would have two representatives, regardless of population, and then there would be the **House of Representatives**, a large body where seats would be determined by population size.

The Electoral College
Beyond that compromise, there was another debate brewing that needed to be settled. Following Shay's Rebellion, there were members of the delegation, among them James Madison, who were becoming disillusioned with the "voice of the people." These delegates argued that the general public was unable to properly make decisions such as who should be president, as most were uneducated. The other side argued that to be a true democracy, the people must decide. This was settled by the **Electoral College**, a system in which there would be a popular vote, but each state would possess delegates equal to the representatives of the House and Senate from that state. Those delegates would then cast the

vote for the president. Select delegates from the states would have the power to reverse a decision, if necessary.

The Three-Fifths Compromise

With those matters resolved, the convention turned its attention to the matter of slavery. Namely, the issue of representation of slaves with regard to population size. The issue of who got to vote was settled (rich, land-owning, white men), but the debate over representation was a census one: women, children, and men were counted. But what about slave states? Northern states, with smaller populations of slaves, argued that slaves shouldn't count at all, while southern states argued that slaves should be counted as full people, just like everyone else. That might sound virtuous, but southern states were seeking larger shares in the representations, with some southern states having slaves representing populations 2:1. The compromise here? The **Three-Fifths Compromise**, a proposal that counted every slave as three-fifths of a person toward representation numbers.

Limitations on Slavery

That wasn't the only compromise reached on slavery. The Founders, split on the issue of slavery, made some movement on the limitation of slavery. In their draft of the Constitution, they outlawed the international slave trade, saying it would become completely illegal beginning in 1808, giving it twenty years. This would eliminate the importation of slaves to the United States, albeit twenty years after the signing of the Constitution. This was easier to swallow for slave states with the aforementioned Three-Fifths Compromise.

Drafting an Amendment Process in Article V

As the final details of the Constitution were being ironed out, many argued about the necessity for changes to the Constitution down the line. Worries over the aging of the document as the United States grew left many within the convention asking questions about how the Constitution would fare over time. With many factors to be considered—such as war, technology, and societal changes—the Framers felt the need to allow the people the option to change the Constitution if need be.

What came next was **Article V**. Article V set the parameters for the people to add amendments to the Constitution. The method the delegates provided was a difficult one, as they intended, so that the government could not work through amendments without the full and unconditional support of the people.

Within Article V, there were two avenues for an amendment to be added. The first was the **congressional proposal method**, which would originate with two-thirds of both chambers of Congress passing an amendment, followed by the state legislatures passing the amendment if three-fourths of the states voted to pass. The second avenue was the **convention method**. This method called for a national convention of the states obtaining two-thirds vote to propose an amendment. Then, three-fourths of special state conventions would need to approve for the amendment to be added. And the process succeeded in being difficult: since the founding, only twenty-seven amendments have been ratified.

Unresolved Issues in the Constitution

Once the Constitution was ratified late in 1788, most of the delegates left the convention satisfied. But as the public debates from Brutus and the necessity of the Federalist Papers show, there were some heavy questions still in the minds of many Americans. Despite ratification, some stark compromises made to get the Constitution ratified, and they have continued to spur debate even today.

Of the most popular, there still lingers the debate over the representation within the Senate. As time has passed and power has landed more heavily within the Senate, some still argue that the two-senator system is a rather poor deal for the larger states, particularly as populations continue to rise in those states. Consider this: California has a population of 39.57 million Americans, or more than ten percent of the U.S. population. Wyoming has a population of 579,315 or one-tenth percent of the U.S. population. Both retain the same voting power in the Senate with two votes apiece. For a chamber that votes on Supreme Court justices and going to war, this seems like quite a bargain.

Further, the most persistent debate left over from the compromise, especially in modern times, is the necessity of the Electoral College system. Recent elections have produced results that perhaps no Framer had quite envisioned. First, in 2000, when Al Gore defeated George W. Bush in the popular vote but lost the electoral vote and the presidency. That was the first and only time such a result occurred until the 2016 election, when the same happened, as Hillary Clinton won the popular vote over Donald Trump despite losing the Electoral College. These results have caused people to question the need for such a system, particularly with so many Americans now plugged into the political system, and with no electoral voters moving away from their state's selections.

Present-Day Constitutional Issues

Despite ratification, there are lingering conversations about the federal government versus state and local governments. Throughout the history of the United States, there have been these squabbles of varying degrees, the most notable example being the Civil War. Even today, prevalent arguments exist about the role of the federal government and the rights of individual citizens in the country.

Constitutional powers of the federal and state government, as well as the individual rights of citizens, are everywhere in today's political climate. One issue that brought them to the forefront is the federal government's handling of security following the 9/11 attacks. The congressional act, known as the **Patriot Act,** appreciably extended the federal government's powers into monitoring its own citizens. Most notably, this included wiretapping, phone hacking, and the development of programs within the National Security Agency to spy on Americans within their own country. This debate came to a head in recent years as whistleblowers let the country know the extent of the programs and people began to push back on the implied intrusion upon their individual freedom.

A more innocuous, yet still important debate, is the role of the federal government in public education. This was sparked following acts in recent years by Congress to attempt to improve education standards. Opponents have cited federal overreach by forcing each state to comply with specific guidelines. They argue that this strips away the states' ability to teach their children and forces them into a federal system. Proponents have argued that it helps standardize test scores and child readiness for higher education within all states, but the limits upon state power are certainly apparent.

These debates are just a few of the constant struggles between the rights of the people and the never-ending battle between state and federal power.

Competing Policy-Making Interests

Separation of Powers and Checks and Balances in the Constitution

With America coming in from both sides of a coin, from too strong of a government by the British to too weak of a government in the Articles of Confederation, the Framers were presented with quite the challenge in drafting the Constitution. Once the real details and compromises had been met and ironed out, the Framers turned their attention to **separation of power**. The biggest point that the Framers were wary of was giving any one body or one person too much power in the new government. To alleviate those concerns, the Framers drafted the Constitution to separate the government into different pieces, each with **checks and balances** over the other.

The **Executive Branch**, consisting of the president and the vice president, was to serve as the Commander and Chief of the armed forces and deal with foreign issues. Also, it was to "execute" or run the government and enforce and enact the laws that Congress passed. The **Legislative Branch**, consisting of the House of Representatives and the Senate, was to be in charge of making all laws for the country. And finally, the **Judicial Branch**, consisting of the court system and the Supreme Court, was to serve as a check over the laws of the nation and provide relief to constitutional questions.

With these constructs for the new government, the Framers made sure to make each branch as independent as possible, while also being sure that one branch could not run over another. This made necessary a system of checks and balances that each branch would hold over another. For example, the legislature can pass and make laws, but the president has veto power. However, the legislature may also override the veto. Additionally, the Supreme Court can review actions and laws by Congress and the president, but the president also appoints to the courts with congressional approval. Congress also approves the budget, so the president can't just do whatever they want to do at any given time.

So, within this system, each branch has specific and established powers that it may use. These powers are also completely independent of the other branches. No branch can be completely out of control, as the other two branches have the ability to provide a check on actions that are extreme or run over another branch of government.

Federalist No. 51

With yet more debate on the horizon as the Framers constructed the Constitution, someone needed to make sense of just exactly what the new system was pushing forward with the checks and balances. Enter James Madison again with his **Federalist No. 51**. Federalist No. 51 was Madison's argument to the people of the reasoning behind the construct of the government, and why the differing branches must have the powers that they were granted.

To understand, Madison made the point that everyone who lived in the United States faced the same political reality, and the same fear: tyranny. Namely, the tyranny of one faction or person within the government controlling too much power. After all, the United States was just a few years removed from a bloody conflict with a tyrant in control of their way of life. For the American people, that reality could never come true again, but it was always close by.

Madison argued that the new construction of government severely limited the ability of such a reality ever happening again. Madison pointed at the differing branches as one facet, arguing that with each possessing independent powers, there were powers that one could attain in a branch that would leave them without access to the power of another. For example, while controlling the presidency would give a faction control over the veto and judicial nominees, there still existed the power of overrides and Supreme Court reviews.

Furthermore, Madison argued that to truly protect the populace from tyranny, the minority must be protected from the majority: the differing aspects of government and governmental entry cured this. With three different branches, each with different subsets of influence, there were fewer opportunities for a large coalition to seize the government completely unchecked. In any instance, there existed at least one other branch of government that could independently check the actions of another. For example, even if a faction took control of the legislature and the presidency, the Supreme Court still had the power of judicial oversight and review.

Madison recognized the concerns of Americans putting their faith in this system. In Federalist No. 51, he argued that the differing opinions and perspectives of the American electorate all but assured that these different parts of the American identity would prevent one faction from dominating public life. But, as a deeper safeguard, Madison also underlined the power of the legislature. Argued by Madison as being the most in tune with basic Americans (because they were voted on in each electorate), the legislature also possessed the most power with this new design of government. They have the power to override the president's veto and to approve the appointees to the Supreme Court and other offices, as well as the normal powers to craft and create the law of the land.

Madison also underscored how careful the Framers had been to level the notion of a too powerful legislature. Within the new constitutional designs, the legislature was given a direct democratic aspect through the House of Representatives being elected by the people, and a more elite democratic aspect in the Senate, with the representatives appointed by state legislatures. This, Madison argued, further ensured against the domination by one faction in the population.

Access Points to Influence Public Policy

While the parameters established for the differing branches of government established some clear lines and protections for the type of tyranny that worried the Framers, it was also important for the Constitution to provide necessary **access points** for the people to join in on governmental affairs. Access points, as the Framers intended them, were points in which the people could influence change at both at the state and federal level of the new government.

The new structure of government provided these access points in a variety of ways. The most important of was the election of their representatives to the House of Representatives and the state legislature. The House being self-explanatory, and the state legislature being important not just for their local government, but also in selecting those who would appoint their Senate leaders.

Further related to Congress was the many ways that voters could influence Congress. One such way was through town halls and protests, which would be protected in the new Constitution. This would give voters a way to stay in touch with their representatives and have a new voice. Beyond that, there existed different interest groups and, more recently, lobbying to advance certain interests vital to a subset of Americans. Influencing and voting on Congress would give voters direct ways to influence and vote in lawmakers who would represent their interests by voting on issues in a way that would suitable for their voting interest.

Another example of influence was the voting method for the president. Voters would have the ability to vote to select their executive, giving them access points even beyond Congress. The president would have the power to appoint judges and other members of government that could influence the way people vote. By voting in a president with likeminded viewpoints on policy issues, voters could influence who sits on key judicial seats and have an executive with veto power over congressional acts.

While not fully meeting the guidelines of a direct democracy, the new government laid out by the Constitution gave the people the ability to directly influence some change. The government as a whole was meant to be a slow process, especially the legislating body. However, through voting, groups of people still possessed the ability to impress upon the system real change and real action, not being at the mercy of representatives they voted in once every two, four, or six years.

Impeachment and Removal of Public Officials Who Abuse Their Power

The Constitution that the Framers drafted seemingly anticipated everything in terms of preventing a corrupt and tyrannical government seizing control over the early Americans. But what about the situation of a single corrupt or criminal member of the government? For this, the Constitution laid out the **impeachment** power.

Given to the legislature, the impeachment power provided a governmental check over officials in both the executive and judicial branches of government. The impeachment power granted Congress the right to review members of other branches to determine if they had violated their oath of office or had committed violations that constituted their removal from office. This important power created a check within the system to remove a person abusing power from office.

The system is complicated. First, for a trial to impeach to begin, the House of Representatives must bring a formal accusation upon the individual. This accusation, secured by a simple majority, or fifty percent plus one vote in the House of Representatives, is what is known as the impeachment. However, this is not the full process; it is merely the accusation that a crime or impeachable offense has been committed.

After the impeachment verdict, the trial heads over to the Senate for the **removal** portion. In the Senate, a two-thirds vote is needed to remove the person from office. The most popular representation of this, the presidential impeachment, has only happened twice in the nation's history and has never resulted in removal from office. In both cases, the Senate did not have enough votes to remove. So, while impeached, both presidents remained in office.

A difficult bar to reach, this two-thirds requirement also guarantees that a faction cannot simply use the impeachment process to remove the executive any time they get a simple majority within the houses of Congress. The Framers made sure that even with this power, there was a path to prevent its abuses by the majority party in the legislature.

Constitutionalism

The Balance of Power Between National and State Government

Among the still-debated topics of today embedded within the Constitution is the never-ending struggle between state and federal governments. The Framers knew that this specific distribution of powers would be the most defining and lasting of the Constitution, and made sure to try to best distribute this power evenly.

Now, as the United States is constructed, there exists a plethora of layers to the government system. There is the federal government, the state government, and a mix of county and local city governments. The system is large and diverse at each level. And each level, particularly the state and national levels, has specific **exclusive** powers. These powers are possessed by that level alone and cannot be interfered with by the other levels of government.

To illustrate, at the federal level, only the national government has the ability to create currency. Also, the purview of foreign affairs falls to the national government, so only it can declare wars and raise an army. The federal government also has complete control of the immigration system, i.e., who gets to come here, who gets to travel abroad, etc.

At the state level, the government has exclusive powers that aren't interfered with by the federal government. State governments have the power of elections, and control all aspects of the election process, even for presidential elections. This means redistricting, vote counts, and sending delegates to the Electoral College all fall to the state. In addition, the state also has the power of setting up county and city governments, overseeing all that happens within the state. Perhaps most importantly, the state has the final say on constitutional amendments, as state votes determine whether an amendment is approved.

The powers of each level sometimes overlap and join together in places, called **concurrent** powers. Chief among these powers that both levels of government control is the power of taxation. For example, both federal and state taxes can be levied on a person or products. Additionally, both levels of government have the power to construct court systems, as well as establish law enforcement divisions. They both may also charter banks and borrow money for debt obligations or new projects within the state or country.

However, this is only the beginning. As time has progressed in the United States, differing parts of the federal and states' concurrent and exclusive powers have changed and begun to overlap even further. As we've moved into current times, these lines between governments have gotten harder to pinpoint.

Grants and Programs that Assist in Changes to Society's Needs on the State and Federal Level

As time has progressed, the needs and demands of society changed. One way the federal government and states have tried to assist with those changes is through grants, incentives, and aid programs aimed at targeting specific areas of interest and parts of society, such as education, transportation, and healthcare, just to name a few.

As touched on previously, the web between the federal and state governments has become quite tangled as the country has gotten older. A main reason for this is the move by the federal government to be more involved in powers normally reserved for the states. So how has this changed happened over time?

One of the easiest ways the federal government has moved in on the states, and one of the more well know, is through **grants**. There are differing types of grants, starting with a **block grant**. Block grants are simply when the federal government gives the state a set amount of funds with a broad goal. For example, the federal government could gift the state of Nevada with a block grant designated to improve infrastructure. The people of Nevada could then use this money broadly in the way they see fit to improve infrastructure in their state.

The other form of grant that is more widely practiced is the **categorical grant**. This type of grant is when the federal government gives a grant to a state with specific guidelines on how the funds are to be used or obtained. This is the form of influence the federal government most often takes to influence the way a state may govern. To give an example, the federal government might designate money to a state to fund education, but it might say that to receive these funds, the state must comply with Common Core guidelines in classrooms. This isn't explicitly forcing the state to comply to Common Core, but not doing so means rejecting the funding. This type of grant is used all of the time in America today.

Along those same lines, there is a **mandate**. A mandate is when the federal government ties funding for the state into guidelines on something else. For example, the government could pass a law banning sales of firearms to those under the age of 18 but within that law tie in money for afterschool programs. So, a state could choose not to enforce the law but doing so would risk losing money for afterschool programs, a seemingly unrelated issue.

And the other way the federal government can influence matters within a state is through **federal revenue sharing**. This is simply the federal government's management of taxes collected that are allocated to the states. With control of this system, the federal government can give money to, and take money away, from states seemingly at will, making it easier to set guidelines for, and guidance over, the states on a variety of issues.

The Tenth and Fourteenth Amendments

The debate between state and federal governments was one that started at the earliest meetings between delegates charged with drafting the Constitution. Certain state advocates were already leery of allowing so much power to a centralized government, and sought safeguards against this within the Constitution. The 9th and 10th Amendments specifically sought to alleviate those worries, but the most common one used is the 10th Amendment.

Added by Madison, the **10th Amendment** states: "The powers not delegated to the United States by the Constitution, nor prohibited by it to the States, are reserved to the States respectively, or to the people." So what does this mean? Well, when addressing the United States, the passage means the federal government. In summary, the 10th Amendment says that powers not granted to the federal government in the Constitution fall to the states.

While this may seem fairly clear-cut, it gets murkier with the **14th Amendment**, which guarantees rights to citizens in each state based on their national rights, which further strengthens federal over state. How did it do this? The 14th Amendment was created as the set of amendments added as a response to the Civil War and slavery. This new amendment established that individual citizens had protection of the federal government from states that treaded on their rights established in the Constitution.

However, these Amendments aren't the only parts of the Constitution that resulted from the debate between federal and state government. The **commerce clause**, a part of Article I of the Constitution, guarantees Congress the power to regulate interstate commerce. This means that Congress can control all buying and selling done between the states, giving Congress quite a large leash to attach to state governments.

This brings the debate to **enumerated powers**. These are the powers of Congress that are expressly granted within the Constitution. For example, they include creating taxes, regulating commerce, handling foreign affairs, borrowing and making money, chartering banks, maintaining an army, declaring war, and making laws. These powers are granted clearly in the Constitution and are the unquestioned powers of Congress. However, this is not where the power of Congress ends.

In Article I, Congress is granted what is called the "necessary and proper" clause, saying Congress shall have the power to "make all laws which shall be necessary and proper for carrying out into execution the foregoing powers." Simply put, Congress has additional powers to what is stated in the Constitution expressly. These powers are called **implied powers**. An example of is that if Congress can create taxes, it can also then create a department and pay people to collect the taxes.

Enumerated powers are straightforward and plain. Implied powers, however, leave open to interpretation what is "necessary and proper," where the power of Congress begins and ends, and where the states versus federal right debate will end up on any given domain issue. That debate, predictably, would play out over the next century.

Court Cases that Demonstrate the Changing Balance of Power Between National and State Governments Over Time

As the infighting between the state and federal governments has reached highs throughout American history, the referee to this situation has been the Supreme Court. Established as the check over Congress and their power, the Supreme Court began rather slowly as the nation started growing, but as tensions were rising early with overlaps in state and federal power, the Supreme Court was increasingly called to settle conflicts between the two governments on a variety of issues, mostly consequential. Then came McCulloch v. Maryland.

McCulloch v. Maryland is a landmark early case that pitted the state of Maryland (and with it, the other states of the Union's interests) versus the federal government, specifically the Second Bank of the United States. In 1816, Congress, facing some money issues following the War of 1812, chartered the Second Bank of the United States. This was a controversial move, as the different states didn't want this bank within their borders, as protection and taxes did not apply to federal banks. But Maryland took the bank in 1816. Two years later, in protest, the state of Maryland imposed a tax on the bank in an effort to move it from Maryland. The cashier of the bank, James McCulloch, refused to pay the tax. The state court decided the bank was unconstitutional because the Constitution said nothing about a federal bank; therefore, Congress did not have the authority to establish one.

Enter the Supreme Court. The state of Maryland laid out its case that the federal government had overstepped. Now, there were two questions for the Supreme Court to answer:

1. Did Congress have the authority to establish a national bank under the Constitution?
2. Did the state of Maryland have the power to tax the bank?

These questions would both be answered in the federal government's favor. Chief Justice Marshall argued in a landmark decision that Congress absolutely had the power to establish a national bank. Marshall argued that despite not being granted the enumerated power to do so, the necessary and proper clause granted Congress the ability to do so. This was the birth of the implied powers. Marshall argued that if there was an end to what Congress sought to do, the means were justified. Furthermore, Marshall argued that Congress was not explicitly forbidden from doing it, so therefore, it was constitutional.

On the second question, the Court again found for Congress. Marshall argued that Maryland's tax on the bank violated the federal government's **supremacy**, saying that federal law superseded state law and could not be interfered with. Marshall argued in the decision, "If the States may tax one instrument, employed by the government in the execution of its powers, they may tax any and every other instrument … This was not intended by the American people. They did not design to make their government dependent on the States."

This ruling would usher in a wave of federalism that was pointed toward federal supremacy over the states and would dominate the better parts of the nineteenth and twentieth centuries.

Toward the end of the twentieth century, however, there began to be a shift back toward the reestablishment of states' powers. Courts began reaffirming states' powers following the New Deal in the 1940s and continued the trend. Congress, for the better part of two centuries, would use the commerce clause as justification for laws all over the spectrum, many over state law. That would begin to change with 1995s *US v. Lopez*.

In 1990, Congress passed the Gun-Free School Zone Act. This act made having a firearm on school grounds illegal. Alfonso Lopez, a student in a Texas high school, took a concealed gun to school, leading to arrest. At trial, his lawyers argued that the law itself is unconstitutional, saying that Congress doesn't have the power to outlaw guns in schools. The federal government argued that Congress does have the power, citing interstate commerce powers. This was challenged with the argument that tying something as disconnected as guns in schools to commerce would mean that almost anything could be tied to commerce.

The Supreme Court looked at the case and decided in Lopez's favor. Chief Justice Rehnquist made the argument that to decide in the federal government's favor would mean that almost anything could be tied to commerce. This would give the federal government the power to police almost anything and would eliminate the boundaries on the federal government's intersection with state lawmaking. The court pushed back and started the trend of walking back some of the federal government's powers that cut into the states' powers, reaffirming a balance.

The Policymaking Process

Within the lawmaking process, the government is a massive web at both the state and federal level. But there are still many ways for those in the community to influence policy and lawmaking. With so many access points—from local, county, state, and federal levels of government—there are many ways to have an impact policy at different levels.

The most common process is a five-step method called the **Policymaking Process**. The first step of this process is the **agenda-setting** stage. This is the part of the process where an issue or a cause that needs attention is identified. The second step is the **policy formulation**. This entails coming up with a proposal to fix the problem. The third step is **policy adoption** or **policy legitimatization**. This is where the campaign to fix the issue begins. This may be through a petition, or community engagement, or writing to a House representative, or any other kind of way to get the issue noticed. The fourth step is the most recognizable part of the process: **policy implementation**. This is the part of the process where a plan comes into place. There is an important final step: **policy assessment**. This is where the solution is examined to see if the policy succeeded, failed, or brought up new issues to address.

Constraints on National Policymaking

In the United States, branches of government are constantly at odds with each other, and state versus federal problems and squabbles are common, yet this is how the Framers intended things to be. The policymaking and lawmaking of the country is supposed to be difficult. The branches are supposed to be at odds so that they may provide a check over each other at all times. The process is a complicated and frustrating one, but that is how it is meant to be.

Practice Questions

1. Which of these choices BEST describes a participatory democracy?
    a. A system in which only the educated and wealthy members of society vote and decide upon the leaders of the country
    b. A system in which groups come together to advance certain select interests
    c. A system that emphasizes everyone contributing to the political system
    d. A system in which one group makes decisions for the population at large

2. With which of the following statements would the author of Brutus No. 1 MOST agree?
    a. A strong central government would be better equipped to protect the rights of the minority
    b. A republican government would more easily control the "mischiefs of factions"
    c. A central republic cannot be an effective government for a nation that is so large in scope
    d. Multiple branches of government provide a safeguard against tyranny by splitting power among differing wings of power

3. Which of the following was NOT a problem presented by the Articles of Confederation?
    a. Infighting between branches of government
    b. The inability to implement and collect taxes to pay off debt
    c. Slow responses from the government toward rebellions
    d. Ineffective raising of armies for wartime

4. Which of the following is NOT one of the checks that individual branches have over another branch of government?
    a. The president may veto a bill passed by Congress
    b. The Supreme Court can try and remove the president for high crimes and misdemeanors committed in office
    c. Congress must approve all of the president's appointments to the Supreme Court
    d. Congress can pass a budget that limits what the president has to spend on defense

5. Upon drafting the Constitution, which part of government did the Framers designate as the part MOST in touch with everyday Americans?
    a. The Senate
    b. The president
    c. The Supreme Court
    d. The House of Representatives

6. Which of the following is not covered under one of the federal government's enumerated powers?
    a. Borrowing money to pay off debt from a war abroad
    b. Passing a law to place a tax on sodas
    c. Banning the possession of firearms in churches
    d. Passing regulations on the sale of California grapes to other states

Read the following scenario and answer the accompanying question.

Congress wants to see changes in the way science is taught in a number of southern states to middle school students. They also know that many southern states have been lobbying Congress for an increase in money for agricultural subsidies within various different fields for farmers in their states. Congress decides to pass a law granting an increase in funding for farming subsidies within those states, but as a stipulation to receiving those funds, states must have their schools teach science by a new guideline drafted by the Department of Education.

7. What type of method has Congress used in this situation to influence the states into doing what Congress wanted?
    a. Block grant
    b. Mandate
    c. Categorical grant
    d. Federal revenue sharing

Read the following scenario and answer the accompanying question.

Walking to school one day, you realize that a main red light near the school that you use to cross the street doesn't have a spot for cross walkers. This causes you to be late to school unless you leave very early in the morning. You come up with a proposal to create a crosswalk at the intersection. You come up with a petition and have decided to go around at lunch and get signatures before you present it to the city council.

8. What stage in the policymaking process are you currently in?
    a. Agenda-setting
    b. Policy legitimization
    c. Policy adoption
    d. Policy formulation

9. Which of the following was NOT one of the compromises made in the Connecticut Compromise?
    a. A lower House of Representatives that is to be selected based on population size
    b. An Electoral College to give delegates a chance to intervene in the event of a wrong choice by the electorate
    c. A Senate consisting of two representatives from each state
    d. A Supreme Court with nine justices to prevent any ties during voting

10. Federalism is described as the contract between the federal government and which of the following?
    a. The people
    b. State governments
    c. The branches of government
    d. The Constitution

Answer Explanations

1. C: A participatory democracy in its truest form is a system in which everyone participates in the political system. Choice *A* describes an elite democracy, which was advocated by some of the Framers like James Madison. Choice *B* is a pluralist democracy—one where interest groups and advocacy for certain issues dominates the government. Choice *D* is the exact opposite of a democracy; it is what the colonies just fought a war to get themselves out of.

2. C: Brutus No. 1 is the famous anti-federalist work that first spurned the Federalist Papers, a response that questioned the new government. Choice *C* highlights this worry with one of the main points that the central government could not effectively govern a nation so large and vast. Choices *A*, *B*, and *D* are all points that are argued in the Federalist Papers by James Madison as a response to Brutus.

3. A: Despite all of the issues of the Articles of Confederation, infighting among the governmental branches was not one of them. This was mainly because there weren't many branches of government, but also because the federal government didn't meet very often. Problems with debt, slow military response, and an army were all problems of the Confederation that prompted the change to a more steadfast and central solution.

4. B: By design, there are many checks and balances among the branches of government. The president does have the power to veto any law passed Congress, which Congress can override. Congress also has the power to consider and approve all of the president's picks for the Supreme Court and federal courts. Congress also controls the budget, which can limit what the president has to spend on the military. However, the Supreme Court does not get to try the president for high crimes and misdemeanors; that job belongs to Congress. The Chief Justice of the Supreme Court, however, does preside over the hearings.

5. D: The Framers (Founding Fathers) had the idea that the higher an office gets, the more out of touch a representative could get from the American people. Members of the Supreme Court are appointed, so they are not the most in touch with everyday Americans. This goes for the Senate and the president as well, as both are elected to longer terms than Representatives. Additionally, the Framers originally set up the Senate such that Senators were chosen by state governments, rather than through direction election by the people. Likewise, the President is voted on by the Electoral College and not by the popular vote of the people.

Members of the House of Representatives are who the Framers had in mind to represent average Americans, both with their small districts and limited terms. Since they face election every two years, they have to consistently think about pleasing their constituents.

6. C: The enumerated powers granted to Congress are the powers that the Constitution directly grants to them. Choice *A* is one of those powers, the power to create and borrow currency. Choice *B* is also one, as it falls under the power of Congress to both pass laws and levy taxes. Choice *D* also falls under the power of Congress to regulate interstate commerce. Choice *C* is not in the enumerated powers and is actually within the parameters of the case of US v. Lopez.

7. B: This problem outlines an issue for Congress where they wish to try and get states to teach something that isn't in the granted powers of the federal government. There are a few methods at Congress's disposal. Choice *A*, a block grant, isn't the right one because Congress would then only be writing a blank check to states hoping they use it to teach the new program. A categorical grant (Choice

C) isn't the right choice either, as this type of grant is when the federal government gives a grant to a state with specific guidelines on how the funds are to be used or obtained. Choice *D*, federal revenue sharing, wouldn't solve the problem. The answer is Choice *B*. A mandate is when Congress uses a law that states want to leverage cooperation on another issue.

8. B: This specific scenario lays out a problem you are facing while trying to go to school. You've noticed the issue, come up with something you think would be a solution, and now you are looking to get people ready to act. Choice *A*, agenda-setting, is incorrect because that is your very first step. Choice *D* can be eliminated because this is the step where you come up with a solution, a part you've already worked through. Choice *C* is the adoption of the policy, which you aren't quite at yet. Choice *B*, policy legitimization, is where you are looking to bring awareness and some muscle to your efforts to get your policy passed.

9. D: The Connecticut Compromise finally eased the tensions of the Constitutional Convention enough to get a deal on the table. Combining the better parts of all of the proposed deals, the compromise was able to get through to become the frame of the new Constitution. Choice *A* (a House of Representatives fixed to population size for representation), Choice *B* (an Electoral College), and Choice *C* (a Senate where each state has exactly two representatives) were all part of the Connecticut Compromise. Choice *D*, the number of justices that currently sit on the court, is not mandated by the Constitution. In reality, there can be as many or as few as Congress wants.

10. B: Federalism, at least how it was put forth by the Framers, is the union between the federal and state governments. While it incorporates the people and the Constitution, the true marriage is the independence of both the states and the federal government.

Unit 2: Interactions Among Branches of Government

Constitutionalism

Functions of the Senate Versus the House of Representatives

The Senate of the United States of America is designed to represents states equally, while the House of Representatives is designed to represent the population. This governmental framework did not take root until the 1787 Constitutional Convention in Philadelphia. Often referred to as the **Connecticut Compromise** or the **Great Compromise** of the 1787 Constitutional Convention in Philadelphia, Pennsylvania, the U.S. Constitution attempted to balance the two major plans for establishing a U.S. legislature: the Virginia Plan (written by James Madison) and the New Jersey Plan (written by William Patterson). The **Virginia Plan** wanted the House of Representatives and the Senate to have congressional seats based on the population of the states. This "proportional right of suffrage" plan, however, would have benefitted larger states more, introducing an inherent inequity in representation (specifically for small states). Small states, like New Jersey, feared the effects of majority rule, so they created the **New Jersey Plan**, which focused on equal legislative representation in the House and the Senate. After much debate, a Great Compromise was forged within the U.S. Constitution—it was decided that the Senate would represent states equally, while the House would be designed to represent the population of each state. Article I, Section 2, Clauses 1-3 of the U.S. Constitution established the representation offered by the House of Representatives: "The House of Representatives shall be composed of members chosen every second year by the people of the several States ... [and] representatives and direct taxes shall be apportioned among the several states which may be included within this Union, according to their respective numbers [i.e., population]." Article I, Section 3, Clause 1 of the U.S. Constitution established the representation offered by the Senate: "The Senate of the United States shall be composed of two Senators from each state, chosen by the Legislature thereof, for six years; and each Senator shall have one vote." Together, these constitutional clauses helped implement the compromises made between advocates of the Virginia Plan and advocates of the New Jersey Plan, establishing our current parameters of U.S. legislative representation.

Formality of Debate is Influenced by Chamber Sizes and Constituencies

The Senate and the House of Representatives are the two chambers of Congress. The Senate is referred to as the **upper chamber of Congress**, while the House of Representatives is referred to as the **lower chamber of Congress**. The district-wide constituencies (i.e., voter groups) represented by the upper chamber of Congress tend to be more homogenous than the state-wide constituencies represented by the Senate. The "one state-two senator formula" established by the Great Compromise afforded a broader representation to the upper chamber of Congress. Regardless of population size, only two senators may represent entire states. This is an extremely difficult endeavor in larger, more populated states such as California and Texas. The diverse populations in these states struggle to maintain appropriate representation in the upper chamber of Congress due to the "one state-two senator formula." The Senate must represent both large and small states, but often struggles to meet the legislative demands of more populated states. Senators, unlike members of the House of Representatives, maintain an equal vote in their chambers—the Senate chamber has a relatively small size in comparison to the House of Representatives. There are currently one hundred senators in the upper chamber, which breaks down to two senators per fifty states. Prior to 1912, all senators were elected by Congress, not by popular vote. Originally, the idea was that senators should represent the state polis rather than popular opinion. Following a constitutional amendment in 1912, all senators are now elected by state-wide popular vote. Nevertheless, due to the close relationship between the House of Representatives and the populous, the lower chamber is still commonly referred to as "the people's chamber" because the House's constituents are district residents rather than state residents. The House of Representatives has a total of 435 legislators (a number established by law in 1911). Each state is entitled to at least one representative in the lower chamber. The number of representatives shifts according to population trends per census. Below is the allocation of congressional districts following the 2010 census:

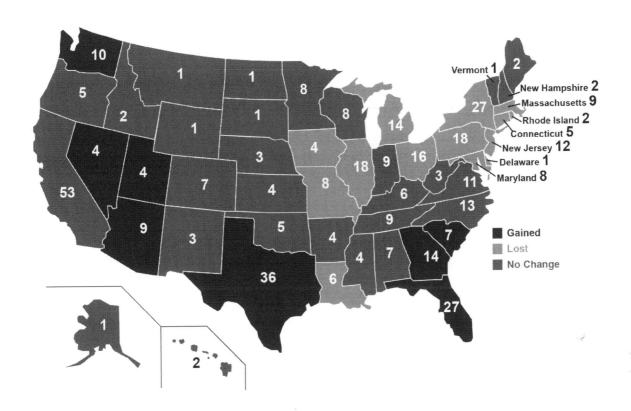

Notice how more populous states like California, Texas, Florida, and New York maintain the most delegates, and, consequently, hold a tremendous amount of legislative power in the lower chamber. Take a look at how many seats are appropriated for these states alone:

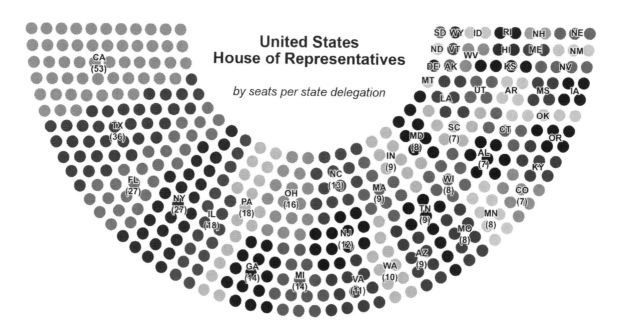

The states with more representatives influence presidential debates and elections because they possess more electoral votes within the Electoral College.

The different sizes and constituencies influence the structural frameworks and operational frameworks of each chamber (including the formality of debate):

	House of Representatives	Senate
Number of Members	435	100
Length of Terms	2 years	6 years
Debate Procedures	Formal	Less formal
Has Filibustering Power	No	Yes
Has Holding Power	No	Yes
Has Rules Committees	Yes	Yes
Has Unanimous Consent Agreements	Yes	No

While debate is less formal in the Senate, senators have more legislative powers (in terms of holding and filibustering bills). Likewise, senators have some unanimous consent agreements when it comes to legislation. The house, which has more formal debate procedures, has no filibustering power, holding power, or unanimous consent agreements.

Congressional Coalitions

Coalitions—which are political groups or alliances that form within each chamber—are inevitably affected by the differing lengths of term for the Senate and the House. The members of the House, or lower chamber, serve two-year terms, while the members of the Senate, or upper chamber, serve six-year terms. Members of the House of Representatives are elected every two years, while two-thirds of the Senate goes up for reelection every two years. Due to these structural and operational differences, the senators of the upper chamber are more likely to form bipartisan coalitions than their counterparts in the lower chamber. Likewise, the house members of the lower chamber are more likely to focus on the legislative necessities of their voting base due to their shorter legislative terms and narrower constituencies.

Congress Creates Public Policies Based on the Enumerated and Implied Powers in the Constitution

With regard to public policy, Congress's expressed or enumerated powers are those that are explicitly stated in Article I, Section 8 of the U.S. Constitution. In addition to the explicit powers, Article I, Section 8, Clause 18 of the U.S. Constitution also affords Congress with a set of additional implied powers. It states that "[Congress shall have the power to] make laws which shall be necessary and proper for carrying into execution the foregoing powers, and all other powers vested by this Constitution in the government of the United States or in any department or officer thereof." Sometimes referred to as the **Elastic Clause**, the **Sweeping Clause**, or the **Necessary and Proper Clause**, these implied powers have allowed Congress to implement wide-ranging policies otherwise not listed directly in the U.S. Constitution. Below is a chart listing the enumerated and implied powers of Congress:

Enumerated Powers of Congress	Implicit Powers of Congress
<ul><li>Making Laws</li><li>Amending the Constitution</li><li>Power of the Purse (i.e., Levying Taxes)</li><li>Declaring War and Maintaining Armed Forces</li></ul>	<ul><li>Regulating Interstate Commerce (according to McCulloch v. Maryland)</li><li>Gun Control Laws</li><li>Federal Minimum Wage</li><li>Income Tax</li><li>The Military Draft</li><li>Environmental Protections (i.e., pollution restrictions and animal conservation efforts)</li></ul>

Passing a Federal Budget, Raising Revenue, and Coining Money

Article I of the Constitution establishes Congress as the primary financial and governmental authority when it comes to passing a federal budget, raising revenue, and coining money. In Article I, Section 9, Clause 7, Congress is defined as the ultimate authority in passing a budget: "No money shall be drawn from the treasury, but in consequence of appropriations made by law; and a regular statement and account of receipts and expenditures of all public money shall be published from time to time." Likewise, Article 1, Section 7, Clause 7 defines and separates duties between the House of Representatives and the Senate when it comes to creating and amending all bills for raising revenue, ensuring that all bills raising revenue originate in the House of Representatives but must be confirmed by the Senate. However, once the House and the Senate agree on passing a particular bill for raising revenue, it must also go through the President, who can veto the bill, unless a two-thirds vote from Congress resurrects it as law. Article I, Section 8, Clause 5 of the U.S. Constitution also makes Congress the authority on the coinage of money: "[The Congress shall have power to] coin money, regulate the value thereof, and of foreign coin, and fix the standards of weights and measures." This article gives Congress the "power of the purse": it is the primary fiscal branch of the U.S. government.

<u>Declaring War and Maintaining the Armed Forces</u>

Article I of the U.S. Constitution also establishes Congress as the primary authority for declaring war and maintaining the armed forces. Article I, Section 8, Clauses 11–18 declare that Congress shall have the power to declare war, raise and support armies/navies, quell rebellions and insurrections, organize and arm militia, create military structures and bases, and make all laws associated with these duties. In essence, Congress is the dominant governmental power when it comes to the military. This was set forth in order to further concentrate federal power.

Enacting legislation that addresses a wide range of economic, environmental, and social issues based on the Necessary and Proper Clause.

The implied powers afforded to Congress by the Elastic Clause, the Sweeping Clause, or the Necessary and Proper Clause, has allowed Congress to historically enact legislation that addresses a wide range of economic, environmental, and social issues without explicit directives in the U.S. Constitution. Congress's role in regulating interstate commerce is, perhaps, the most famous of the implied power to emerge from this clause. The landmark **McCulloch v. Maryland** Supreme Court case confirmed that the U.S. Constitution implicitly allows Congress to maintain the power to create a federal bank within state lines and enact taxes. Since 1927, Congress has maintained the power to pass laws that limit the possession and sale of firearms. This controversial gun control power has led to a firestorm of political debates throughout American history. Likewise, since passage of the Revenue Act of 1861, Congress has had the power to levy an income tax, and, since the passage of the Federal Minimum Wage Act in 1938, Congress has also had the power to set a national minimum wage. The Elastic Clause has allowed Congress's powers to expand dramatically since the U.S. Constitution was created. Congress now has the authority to control areas as wide-ranging as pollution/conservation (i.e., environmental protection) and the military draft.

The Differences Between the U.S. Senate and House of Representatives on the Policy-Making Process

The Senate and the House of Representatives have different structures, powers, and functions in the policy-making process, as granted by the implicit and explicit powers established the U.S. Constitution. The different structures and functions of the U.S. Senate and U.S. House of Representatives inevitably affect the decision-making process for government policy. The separate structures, powers, and functions the U.S. Senate and U.S. House of Representatives ensure not only that legislation is "checked and balanced," but also some structures, powers, and functions favor one side of the legislative branch over the other. For example, according to the Constitution, legislation focusing on treaties and appointment confirmations must be debated and heard in the Senate. This gives the Senate a natural advantage over the House of Representatives when it comes to foreign policy.

Constitutional Responsibilities of the House and Senate

Both the Senate and the House of Representatives rely on committees to investigate, amend, or strike down bills. These committees have different rules and different roles based on what chamber they emerge in. Committees in the upper chamber (the Senate) have different rules than committees in the lower chamber (the House of Representatives). These committees also have specific constitutional responsibilities. Legislation focusing on treaties and appointment confirmations are the responsibility of Senate committees. Congressional actions focusing on impeachment and tax/revenue bills are investigated first by committees in the House of Representatives. While impeachment begins in the House of Representative, the person being impeached will be tried in the Senate.

Chamber-Specific Procedures, Rules, and Roles

Here is a list of general chamber and debate rules that must be followed within the Senate:

- Legislation and appointments typically go to committees for reviews and revisions.

- Legislation and appointments can be taken to hearings for further investigation.

- For treaties and appointments, a two-thirds supermajority vote is needed in the Senate.

- For general legislation, a fifty-one-vote majority is needed in the Senate.

- If the Senate chooses to debate a bill, the debate can end only with unanimous consent.

- If the debate is not going the way one group expected, they can place the bill on hold and create a filibuster.

- A filibuster can be ended only with a sixty-vote cloture.

- Filibusters related to appointments can be ended with just a fifty-one-vote cloture.

Here is a list of general chamber and debate rules that must be followed within the House:

- Impeachment proceedings and tax/revenue bills are initiated in the House of Representatives.

- Committees in the House of Representatives, just like in the Senate, can choose not to bring a bill to vote.

- A discharge petition can force a bill onto the floor through a majority vote.

- The House of Representatives is much more hierarchical and centralized than the Senate.

- There are no filibusters, unanimous consent, or holding powers in the House of Representatives.

A bill introduced in the House of Representatives first goes to the Speaker of the House, who then chooses a committee to review and revise the bill. At this point, the Rules Committee gets involved. The committee then can choose to either bring the bill to a hearing or a debate on the House floor. The Rules Committee decides the rules of the debate. In some cases, the bill will be debated as a **Committee of the Whole**, which is a very large committee that decides whether a bill should be voted on. If a bill is placed on hold at any point in this process, a discharge petition can force a bill onto the floor through a majority vote.

Certain legislative leaders within these chambers take on specific roles and responsibilities that assist with legislative operations. Below is a list of chamber-specific roles that are common within Congress:

Role	Responsibilities
President of the Senate	The President of the Senate helps preserve order in the upper chamber by presiding over daily sessions, stating parliamentary motions, referring bills to committees, and acting as the legislative spokesperson for the upper chamber.
President pro tem of the Senate	The President pro tem of the Senate is second-in-command, presiding over functions in the president's absence and assuming any other duties delegated by the president.
Majority Leader	The Majority Leader speaks on behalf of the majority party in the chamber during debates. The Majority Leader also assists with programmatic aspects of the chamber, developing a calendar when necessary.
Minority Leader	The Minority Leader represents the minority.
Speaker of the House	The Speaker of the House assumes all functions of the President of the Senate, but within the context of the lower chamber.
Speaker pro tem	The Speaker pro tem is second-in-command, presiding over functions in the Speaker of the House's absence and assuming any other duties delegated by the Speaker of the House.
Majority Whip	The Majority Whip assists the debate floor leader by ensuring attendance, counting votes, and continuously communicating the majority position.
Minority Whip	The Majority Whip assists the minority leader by ensuring attendance, counting votes, and continuously communicating the minority position.
Majority Caucus Chair	The Majority Caucus Chair develops the agenda for the majority, presiding over caucus meetings.
Minority Caucus Chair	The Minority Caucus Chair assists the minority platform by presiding over caucus meetings.

Instead of deciding to carry out hearings or debates, the Senate can choose to table a bill. When a bill is **tabled**, it enters a sort of legislative limbo where it can either be amended, resurrected, or killed altogether.

If the bill enters into a Senate debate, the debate cannot be ended until there is unanimous consent. Every single one of the one hundred U.S. senators must agree to end the debate. If one senator chooses to not end the debate, the debate will be placed on hold.

A **filibuster** is the term for a protracted debate on the Senate floor. The word is used to explain those persons who want to hold up the legislation. Filibusters are usually carried out by a minority group of detractors who want to impede the legislative process in hopes that the bill will be stopped in its tracks. The only way to defeat a filibuster is with a cloture. For general legislation, sixty votes must exist in order to end a filibuster with a cloture. This is different than the normal fifty-one votes needed to pass general legislation. For executive appointments, only fifty-one votes are needed for a cloture.

Only the Senate (and not the House of Representatives) is involved in ratifying treaties. The president has the power to sign a treaty, but the treaty does not become binding until a two-thirds Senate supermajority ratifies it. The Senate's role in treaty ratification ensures that it has more influence over foreign relations than the House of Representatives. Likewise, the Senate is also involved in confirming appointments. The president has the power to declare appointments for executive or judiciary positions, but the Senate has the authority to confirm these appointments.

Developing the Federal Budget

According to the U.S. Constitution, Congress is the governmental branch responsible for establishing a budget for the federal government. Throughout this budgetary process, Congress must consider two types of federal spending: discretionary spending and mandatory spending. **Discretionary spending** uses roughly one-third of the federal budget for appropriations costs, which are established by Congress every fiscal year, beginning on October 1. Discretionary spending accounts for most of the direct activities initiated by the federal government, including defense programs, educational programs, and national security programs. Discretionary spending, historically, has continued to grow, accounting for about one trillion dollars of the federal budget. This has been the focus of many recent political debates over fiscal responsibility. **Mandatory spending** entails all of the other spending enacted by the federal government (which does not have to go through appropriations legislation). This spending includes entitlement programs such as Social Security and Medicare. This type of spending accounts for two-thirds of the federal budget. Thus, as entitlement costs grow, spending opportunities will decrease unless either tax revenues increase or the budget deficit decreases. The budget deficit, however, has continued to expand as both entitlement costs and discretionary spending have increased over the past twenty years.

Pork Barrel Legislation and Logrolling

Pork barrel legislation, or **pork barrel politics**, occurs when legislators utilize federal government funds to finance local government projects that benefit loyal political constituents or potential political constituents. Traditionally, the funding used for pork barrel legislation projects draws on taxes or funds from a larger geographic pool of constituents but is only used to enhance projects within a smaller constituency. Pork barrel legislation can both directly and indirectly affect lawmaking in both chambers. It can directly affect legislation by creating coalitions and campaign contributions that cater to the needs of particular constituents or constituencies. It can also directly affect the democratic process by swaying voting blocs. Many citizens and lawmakers criticize pork barrel legislation because it advances the intersectionality of money and politics, paving the way for historically corrupt political machines such as the Tammany Hall machine in New York. Sometimes pork barrel legislation indirectly affects lawmaking by encouraging logrolling, a process by which legislators vote for pork barrel legislation even if it does not directly benefit their own constituents. Logrolling, however, can help these politicians win support for their own political agendas and initiatives.

Factors that Influence Congressional Behavior and Governing Effectiveness

Ideological Divisions Within Congress

Congressional behavior and governing effectiveness are often influenced by ideological divisions within Congress that can lead to gridlock or create the need for negotiation and compromise.

The behavior and effectiveness of Congress are influenced by ideological divisions (or unifications). If Congress is ideologically split along political lines, it makes it difficult to pass legislation that needs a supermajority vote. Political divisions can gridlock, or even shut down, the government, as recently illustrated by the debate over border security during the Trump Administration. The only way to bypass a gridlock or shutdown is to either kill the legislation or negotiate/compromise.

Gerrymandering, Redistricting, and Unequal Representation of Constituencies

Congressional behavior and governing effectiveness are also influenced by gerrymandering, redistricting, and unequal representation of constituencies.

Gerrymandering is the practice of using redistricting to gain a political advantage in upcoming elections. **Redistricting** is the process of legally manipulating district boundaries for congressional and state legislative districts (which are reapportioned every ten years following U.S. census results). Redistricting should be used to create equal representation amongst constituencies; however, the practice of gerrymandering has often created unequal representation. Two major Supreme Court decisions have influenced the ways in which the United States addresses challenges to gerrymandering, redistricting, and unequal representation of constituencies: *Baker v. Carr* (1961) and *Shaw v. Reno* (1993).

Baker v. Carr (1961) established the precedent that the Supreme Court has the authority to review redistricting issues at the local level, which had previously been deemed "political questions that existed outside the jurisdiction of the judicial branch." The court case also established the "one person, one vote standard" that affords equal protection by granting that one person's voting power should carry the same weight as another person's voting power within a single state. *Shaw v. Reno* (1993) resulted from complaints made by a contingent of white voters in North Carolina who were upset about recent redistricting efforts that created two "majority-minority" districts in the state. Citing protections made by the Fourteenth Amendment, the Supreme Court agreed that racial categories cannot be the sole driving force for creating or realigning districts.

Elections That Have Led to a Divided Government

Presidential and midterm elections—and the political ideologies that they pit against each other—can divide governments, pitting presidential platforms against partisan congressional initiatives. For instance, if the presidency is defined by a Republican ideology, but Congress is dominated by Democrats, it can create a vitriol political climate in which Congress refuses to work with the president (and vice versa). In worst case scenarios, these divided governments can block presidential appointments to executive branch agencies and cabinets and/or lead to "**lame duck**" presidencies in which Congress is already focused on meeting the demands of the presidential successor rather than carrying out the initiatives of the sitting president (i.e., the lame duck).

Different Role Conceptions of "Trustee," "Delegate," and "Politico"

Legislators generally assume certain political roles that both reflect and affect the relationships of accountability that they have with their constituents. Four prominent roles (or legislative leadership types) dictate the voting patterns of each legislator. Legislators who envision themselves as **trustees** of the communities they serve assume that votes must be decided on a case-by-case basis, independent of party affiliation or constituent pressure. Party ideology might influence the decision-making process, but it will not dictate it. Legislators who see themselves as **delegates** to their communities make voting decisions based on what they believe the constituents in their state or district want. Delegates envision themselves as the legislative agents of the communities. **Partisan politicians** vote based on their party affiliations; they follow the decisions of the party as a whole. Lastly, a **politico** is a politically savvy person who incorporates key aspects of being a trustee, delegate, and partisan politician in order to maintain cordial relationships with all stakeholders. Some might call a politico a true politician in the sense that they are always trying to please a diversity of stakeholders.

Presidential Powers

The executive branch, like Congress, possesses both formal and informal powers to accomplish the office's policy agenda. Formal powers are explicitly stated in Article II of the U.S. Constitution. Informal powers are implicitly allowed by the U.S. Constitution, namely the Elastic Clause, but not explicitly stated. Generally speaking, U.S. presidential power has expanded throughout American history, thanks in large part to the invocation of these informal powers. Following the New Deal presidency of Franklin Delano Roosevelt in the 1930s and 1940s, the U.S. presidency has increased its role in government through executive orders and agreements. A list of formal and informal powers claimed by all U.S. presidents are listed below:

Formal Powers of the Presidency	Informal Powers of the Presidency
• Military Power as Commander-in-Chief: Hoping to prevent a military coup by an armed forces general, the Framers of the U.S. Constitution deemed the president, a civilian, as the "Commander in Chief," which granted him the military power to mindfully check and balance the potentially-dangerous power of the armed forces. • Diplomatic Treaty Power with Foreign Nations: The president is the only government official who can sign treaties, but only if given consent by two-thirds of the Senate. Any treaty that is not signed by the president is considered void. • Appointment/Selection Powers: While the Senate gives advice and consent to all executive appointments/selections, it is ultimately the president's formal duty to appoint/select Cabinet members, ambassadors, consuls, Supreme Court judges, White House staff, and public ministers.	• Executive Orders: Executive orders are, perhaps, the strongest example of the informal, extraconstitutional powers the U.S. president has been granted throughout the twentieth and twenty-first centuries. Executive orders allow the president to create public policies without the input of Congress. • Signing Statements, Executive Agreements, and Presidential Proclamations: None of these acts needs congressional input. The president has the "power of the pen" here much like with executive orders. • Opposing Nullification: This is not a formal power of the U.S. president, as stated by the U.S. Constitution, but President Andrew Jackson employed this extraconstitutional strategy to strike down the nullification crisis that existed between the federal government and state government of South Carolina in 1832–1833.

- Vetoes: Article I, Section 7 of the U.S. Constitution affords the president of the United States with the authority and right to block bill with veto, sometimes referred to as a regular veto, within ten days of its approval by the originating house of Congress. A regular veto returns an unsigned bill back to the House or the Senate it originated from. It is usually accompanied by some sort of memorandum or veto message that allows the president to explain his disapproval. A two-thirds vote of each house can override a regular veto, which allows the bill to become law regardless of the president's concerns.

- Pocket Vetoes: Article 1, Section 7 of the U.S. Constitution grants the president the power to review a measure passed by Congress within ten days of its passage. If the president retains the bill while Congress is adjourned, then it becomes a pocket veto and the bill does not become law.

- Suspending Habeas Corpus during Wartime: This is not a formal power of the U.S. president, as stated by the U.S. Constitution, but President Abraham Lincoln employed this extraconstitutional tactic to protect the nation during the Civil War.

- Personal Persuasion: Even more informal than the practices listed above, the president can use informal negotiation, indirect lobbying efforts (through White House staff), social media, political rallies, the news media, and town halls/speeches to exert their presidential power and opinion.

- Executive Privilege: The U.S. president, if they so choose, can withhold some executive information from Congress, even though this power is not explicitly declared in the U.S. Constitution.

Conflict Between the Executive Branch and the Senate

As previously mentioned, the U.S. Constitution grants the president with the formal power to appoint/select Cabinet members, ambassadors, consuls, Supreme Court judges, White House staff, and public ministers. However, the Senate ultimately must consent with these appointments/selections. Differing political opinions regarding appointments/selections can result in conflicts between the president (the executive) and Congress (the legislature). Such conflicts can result in committee hearings, such as those used to try to block some of President Donald Trump's appointments/selections following his election to office in 2016. Such conflicts can snowball into larger political bouts between the president and Congress.

Below is a chart explaining each type of executive appointment:

Executive Branch Appointment Type	Definition
Cabinet Members	Article II, Section 2 of the U.S. Constitution established the Presidential Cabinet and its role in advising the president of the United States of America. The current manifestation of the Cabinet includes the vice president of the United States of America, the White House chief of staff, the attorney general, and various cabinet members in other departments and agencies. The positions filled by current Cabinet members include: • Secretary of Agriculture • Secretary of Commerce • Secretary of Defense • Secretary of Education • Secretary of Energy • Secretary of Health and Human Services • Secretary of Homeland Security • Secretary of Housing and Urban Development • Secretary of the Interior • Secretary of Labor • Secretary of State • Secretary of Transportation • Secretary of Treasury • Secretary of Veteran Affairs
Ambassadors	Ambassadors are nominated by the U.S. president to monitor international politics, mediate and consult on international crises, and serve as diplomats to foreign nations around the world. Ambassadors are nominated by the U.S. president and confirmed by the Senate.
Consuls	Consuls are likewise appointed by the U.S. president and confirmed by the Senate. Consuls officially reside in other countries or territories to protect the citizens of one's own country and maintain foreign relations.
Supreme Court Judges	Supreme Court judges serve as the head judicial authorities in the United States; they are appointed by the president for life-long terms, and their appointments are confirmed by the Senate.

White House Staff	There are over three hundred White House staffers who assist the executive office. The most prestigious positions include: • Chief of Staff • Head of the Environmental Protection Agency (EPA) • Administrator of Small Business Administration • Director of National Intelligence • U.S. Trade Representative • Director of the Central Intelligence Agency • Director of the Office of Management and Budget
Public Ministers	"Public ministers" is a blanket term used for any officially-appointed public servant who represents the United States within the international community.

The President's Longest Lasting Influence

The United States government was designed to have certain checks and balances in place to limit the power of the three branches: the executive branch, the legislative branch, and the judicial branch. Throughout relatively modern U.S. history, the executive branch and legislative branch have often participated in a tug-of-war power display. Senate confirmation of presidentially-appointed, life-tenured Supreme Court justices has been one of the main points of contention between the executive and legislative branches. The 2017 appointment of Supreme Court Judge Neil Gorsuch is an example of the potential for contention. The judge's appointment was not unanimously accepted by the U.S. Senate. Instead, the Republican appointee, confronting a mere 52-48 Republic majority in the U.S. Senate, received his commission by a 54-45 vote only after participating in confirmation hearings before the Senate Judiciary Committee. In this scenario, the president positioned his political party to have a longer-lasting influence on American law and politics. Because Supreme Court judges assume life-tenured roles in the American government, they have the opportunity to carry out the policies of their president or party long after a presidential term has ended. A Supreme Court appoint, though meant to balance American government, can potentially create lasting imbalances in American law and government. For instance, if the majority of Supreme Court judges happen to be liberal, then consequently, there is a potential to liberalize American law for a long time. Likewise, if the majority of Supreme Court judges happen to be conservative, then there is the potential to have a lasting conservative impact on American constitutional interpretations and decisions. This makes the president's longest lasting influence the appointment of Supreme Court judges; it is a formal presidential power that has significant consequences.

Presidential Policy Initiatives and Executive Orders Can Conflict with the Congressional Agenda

Unilateral actions promoted by the president, including policy initiatives and executive orders, have historically led to policy changes in domestic and international affairs that circumvent congressional approval and constitutional mandate. The unilateral powers of the executive branch have mushroomed since the 1930s and 1940s, often at the expense of Congress and the Constitution. This consistent escalation of unchecked presidential power has resulted in congressional backlash because it has consistently undermined the congressional agenda. A good example of this political tug-of-war between the legislature and the president occurred in the early 1970s when President Richard Nixon decided to secretly bomb Cambodia, circumventing congressional approval and invoking his role as Commander in

Chief. Congress quickly challenged Nixon's excesses—the War Powers Act of 1973 addressed President Richard Nixon's contested powers as Commander in Chief, limiting the president's ability to deploy military forces. Nevertheless, in the decades that follow, presidents ignored this congressional act, leading to further conflict.

Federalist No. 70 and the Single Executive

In **Federalist No. 70**, author Alexander Hamilton asserted that the executive power is more easily confined when there is one executive rather than many. Essentially, Hamilton argued that once executive power is multiplied, it may be more inclined endanger liberty. According to Hamilton, the multiplication of the executive position could lead to a toxic amount of dissension and disagreement within the executive branch. Hamilton assumed that a strong, singular executive leader is necessary, especially after the feeble federal efforts to multiply power during the era of the Articles of Confederation. He believed a single executive, whose authority can be checked and balance by a Council (i.e., Congress), can strengthen the American republic.

Changing Presidential Roles

The informal powers of the United States president have expanded dramatically throughout the twentieth and twenty-first centuries. Gradually, the power of U.S. presidents, in spite of Alexander Hamilton's call to confine the powers of the president to one, has expanded and multiplied, claiming duties and directives beyond those formal powers explicitly expressed by Article II of the U.S. Constitution. Presidential power is no longer limited by the Constitution; it is no longer even limited to the executive office. With the power invested in social media, appointment processes, presidential traditions, and external associations, the modern-day U.S. presidency has come to represent a multitude of constituents and an array of informal powers. This grand display of extraconstitutional power and the ever-changing role of the president has led to several constitutional-power restrictions in the past one hundred years.

The two most notable of these restrictions include the passage of the Twenty-second Amendment (1951) and the passage of the War Powers Act (1973). Following President Franklin D. Roosevelt's four-term presidency in the 1930s and 1940s, Congress decided to constitutionalize the two-term standard first established by President George Washington. The subsequent **Twenty-second Amendment** (1951) to the U.S. Constitution stated that a president is only allowed to be elected twice and may only serve up to ten years as president (in instances where a vice president or other government official has to assume the role of president without election). The **War Powers Act of 1973** addressed President Richard Nixon's contested powers as Commander in Chief, limiting the president's ability to deploy military forces. This tug-of-war between the legislature and the president has continued to play out since the passage of this act, with many presidents circumventing the act by invoking their role as Commander in Chief.

Different Perspectives on the Presidential Role

Since the inception of the New Deal Order in the 1930s and 1940s, the informal powers of the U.S. president have expanded dramatically, establishing a precedent for a series of unilateral executive orders and actions. Examples of such unilateral actions include President Truman's Korean War, President Johnson's Gulf of Tonkin Resolution, President Nixon's bombing of Cambodia, and President Bush's Terrorist Surveillance Program. Depending on a person's political ideologies or allegiances, they might argue that a more expansive interpretation of presidential power is necessary; they may even claim that this sort of display of unilateral decision-making falls within the responsibilities of the president of the United States' role as the Commander in Chief. Others might view this steady escalation of unchecked presidential power as a direct threat to individual liberty. These differing perspectives on presidential power continue to be reviewed and debated by politicians, journalists, scholars, and common citizens in the United States. This debate generally centers on two points of contention: liberty and security (and the intersection between the two).

The Presidency's Communication Impact

<u>Modern Technology, Social Media, and Rapid Response to Political Issues</u>
The communication impact of the president has evolved to incorporate a variety of modern technologies, which have consequently influenced the "political reach" of the president. The 2008 presidential election marked a monumental transition in the ways in which presidential candidates and government officials use modern technology and social media to interact with everyday citizens. Barack Obama—who defeated John McCain in the 2008 presidential election—is often likened to Franklin Delano Roosevelt and John F. Kennedy for his ability to capitalize on modern technological trends as a campaign medium.

While Franklin Delano Roosevelt became well known for his Fireside Chats on the radio and John F. Kennedy mastered television as a tool for reaching the masses, President Barack Obama is known as the first president to master the art of social media. His campaigns and presidential terms employed useful social media platforms such as Reddit, Twitter, Myspace, YouTube, Facebook, Instagram, Spotify, and Pinterest. He is the first president to ever host a Twitter town hall meeting. Obama used these platforms to advertise, organize supports, and interact with ordinary citizens. Following his success in 2008, President Barack Obama emailed a personalized video to millions of citizens to announce his intention to run for reelection. Likewise, his Republican counterpart, Mitt Romney, announced his intention to run for president on Twitter. Political pundits often point to Obama's inordinate number of "followers" and "friends" on social media as a key to his success.

Following the successful implementation of social media into the Oval Office by Barack Obama, many other grassroots organizations, political parties, politicians, political pundits, lobbyist groups, political action committees (super PACs), and think tanks began to adopt social media platforms as a means to garner support and communicate rapidly with citizens. This paradigm shift has fundamentally changed the ways in which the public interacts with public officials. One of the fundamental pitfalls of utilizing social media as advertising in modern politics is the fact that, unlike newspaper, radio, and television ads, social media allows a variety of stakeholders to interact with the message. They can like or dislike the advertisement, share the advertisement, comment on the advertisement, or even manipulate the advertisement into memes or gifs. Thus, social media campaigns run the risk of attracting negative attention.

Politicians are also turning to the Internet, social media, and mobile apps for fundraising purposes. Democrat Howard Dean, an early adopter of this method of fundraising, is often credited with being one of the first politicians to use the Internet to fundraise for his 2004 presidential election campaign. By 2012, President Barack Obama raised over six hundred million dollars through online fundraising. Bernie Sanders' 2016 campaign broke records, raising over eight million dollars in one day. This new crowdsourcing approach to politics is turning millions of citizens into small-dollar donors, which has consequently disrupted the political reliance on super PACs.

Social media has the capacity to not only create political firestorms, but also communicate in times of crisis. It is a rapid, instantaneous way for presidents to reach out to the citizens in times of political stalemate or national crisis.

Agenda Setting Via Nationally-Broadcast State of the Union Messages and the President's Bully Pulpit

Article II, Section 3 of the United States Constitution is often cited as the reasoning behind the State of the Union Address. It states that the President of the United States "shall from time to time give to Congress information of the State of the Union, and recommend to their consideration such measures as he shall judge necessary and expedient." President George Washing was the first to take advantage of this constitutional clause, delivering the first-ever annual address to Congress on January 8, 1790. President John Adams would follow suit with this tradition, delivering the message by speech to Congress, but Thomas Jefferson chose to break from this tradition, providing his address to Congress in a written format. This Jeffersonian tradition lasted until 1913, when President Woodrow Wilson resurrected the initial Washingtonian approach.

Wilson's presidency marks the beginning of the first modern **State of the Union Address**, which would not receive its modern-day title until President Franklin Delano Roosevelt's paradigm-shifting presidency. The reasoning behind Wilson's resurrection of the Washingtonian approach to the State of the Union is that Wilson believe the nation deserved to visibly see the executive leader of the United States working alongside (or, in front) of its legislative branch. It is a symbolic gesture of both collaboration and power that has been utilized by every modern president except Herbert Hoover. Modern technologies—radio, television, the Internet, and social media—have bolstered this symbolic gesture. As a result of these modern technologies, and the relative expansion of presidential power in the twentieth century, the State of the Union has become even more symbolic—it is an annual event in which the President of the United States gets to set the national and political agenda. It has evolved from a constitutional expectation to a national tradition, one that has the power to move the nation in whatever direction the president chooses.

The first State of the Union Address to be nationally broadcast on the radio was delivered by President Calvin Coolidge on December 6, 1923. Since 1923, the State of the Union Address has been utilized by presidents as a platform for setting national and political agendas, and, at times, it has been used as a bully pulpit to sway political opinions or launch political initiatives. The radio was used to broadcast State of the Union messages throughout the 1920s, 1930s, and 1940s. On January 6, 1947, President Harry Truman became the first president to deliver a State of the Union Address on national television.

Realizing that the new medium of television presented an opportunity to further engage the citizens of the United States of America, the Lyndon B. Johnson Administration decided to move the address from its traditional midday timeslot. In order to reach more citizens "on their own time," the first evening, primetime State of the Union address was delivered by President Johnson on January 4, 1965. Since then, the State of the Union has become a primetime tradition on television, and, with the advent of the Internet, presidents, beginning with George W. Bush in 2002, have also begun streaming the important address on webcasts and other online platforms.

Judicial Branch Powers are Set Forth in Article III of the Constitution

Article III of the Constitution is an extension of Alexander Hamilton's Federalist No. 78, which establishes the foundational powers and duties of the judicial branch of government. According to Federalist No. 78, it is pertinent that the judicial branch of the United States remains independent from Congress to ensure that state and federal legislative bodies remain checked and balanced by the courts.

Uniting the judiciary with the legislative body, in Hamilton's opinion, would allow for unchecked powers that "may poison the foundations of justice." Article III of the U.S. Constitution consequently ensures that the judicial power of the United States is vested in one, independent Supreme Court. By February 24, 1803, in the early years of the American republic, the Supreme Court set the standard for the ways in which Article III would influence U.S. constitutional law. In the landmark decision of **Marbury v. Madison** (1803), Chief Justice John Marshall officially used Article III of the U.S. Constitution to establish the doctrine of judicial review. The case represented the first time that the federal courts summoned their authority to strike down acts of Congress deemed unconstitutional.

The Role of Precedents and *Stare Decisis* in Judicial Decision Making

A Latin phrase that means "to stand by things decided," **stare decisis** is a principle that all U.S. courts, including the Supreme Court, use to make judicial decisions. Because it is a principle, and not a rule, *stare decisis* is not a mandatory practice, but rather a best practice in judicial decision making. *Stare decisis* allows courts to review past judicial decisions, or precedents, particularly those made by the Supreme Court, in order to inform their own judicial decisions. Lower courts are bound by all Supreme Court rulings, but the Supreme Court itself can change past precedents through new judicial decisions. The lower courts, on the other hand, cannot change the precedents made by the Supreme Court, but can be informed by them, and they can also be informed by decisions made by other lower courts of equal rank.

Judicial Appointments Affect Precedents

Judicial appointments to the Supreme Court of the United States have the power to shift entire paradigms of U.S. constitutional law. This is especially true when the general makeup of the Supreme Court is politically and ideologically homogenous. While most U.S. Supreme Courts have remained relatively moderate, there have been times in history when the political leanings of the entire judicial branch have swayed constitutional law, in either a more liberal or conservative direction, in terms of establishing new or rejecting existing precedents. Between 1990 and 2010, the Supreme Court remained relatively balanced yet polarized, with ideologies being split between conservative and liberal agendas.

The Effects of Controversial or Unpopular Supreme Court Decisions

The legislative and executive branches may challenge controversial or unpopular Supreme Court decisions by debating the judicial branch's right to enact judicial review or questioning the validity of their judicial interpretations. One way to address these points of contention is through the Supreme Court justice appointment process. In the wake of a vacancy, the president can choose to appoint a new justice that will likely uphold the opinions of the executive branch and Congress can choose to confirm this role as a reflection of their own ideological preferences. If future appointments are too distant to enact immediate change, Congress can enact legislation that might limit the Supreme Court's power by changing or modifying its jurisdictions or decisions, or by amending the U.S. Constitution. In some rare cases, the president might ignore a Supreme Court decision altogether as President Andrew Jackson did with forced Indian (Native American) removal in the early 1800s.

The Ongoing Debate Over Judicial Activism Versus Judicial Restraint

Judicial restraint and judicial activism are two conflicting theories of judicial interpretation that have been utilized by the Supreme Court and its justices throughout U.S. history. Like all theories, judicial restraint and judicial activism manifest themselves in different ways. Nevertheless, there are two generally-accepted definitions that guide the understanding of Supreme Court justices. **Judicial restraint** requires the Supreme Court to not inject their personal biases or perspectives into the U.S. Constitution, choosing instead to take on the role as strict interpreters of the U.S. Constitution. Consequently, adherents to this theory would defer policy-making decisions to the other political branches of the U.S. government (as long as the policymakers are also strictly adhering to the U.S. Constitution). **Judicial activism** assumes that strict interpretations and noninterventionist approaches to constitutional law can be dangerous, exposing citizens to rights infringements. Judicial activism is therefore the more active and intervention-oriented approach to constitutional law. Advocates of judicial activism believe that the Supreme Court also has the responsibility to protect rights that are not explicitly stated in the U.S. Constitution.

Examples of Restrictions on the Supreme Court

Congressional Legislation to Modify the Impact of Prior Supreme Court Decisions
Congress maintains the right to use legislation as a means to reinterpret, modify, and/or amend the impact of prior Supreme Court decisions by either clarifying their original intent or overruling a Court decision that runs contrary to constitutional law or federal mandates.

Constitutional Amendments
The Supreme Court of the United States is bound by the explicit directives laid out in Article III of the U.S. Constitution. If the Supreme Court is believed to be functioning outside of its constitutional jurisdiction, Congress has the right to limit these excesses by amending the U.S. Constitution and including more explicit restrictions.

Judicial Appointments and Confirmations
Supreme Court judges are not elected officials. Instead, they are appointed by the executive branch (the president) and confirmed by legislative branch (the Senate). The power of the Supreme Court is therefore limited by this appointment and confirmation process. Every single judge must be hand-selected by a president and approved by Congress. These restrictions ensure that the Supreme Court remains checked and balanced by the other branches. Nevertheless, this process, albeit restrictive, can consolidate political power within the judiciary if the majority of judges appointed and confirmed represent one political party or ideology.

The President and States Evading or Ignoring Supreme Court Decisions
Displays of informal powers by the president and/or the states can undermine the formal powers of the judiciary. Evasion of the law or outright disregard for the law can undermine the Supreme Court's strength. Presidents and governors can consciously or unconsciously circumvent legal decisions of the Supreme Court. Abraham Lincoln's suspension of *habeas corpus* during the Civil War is likely the greatest example of a president ignoring the legal parameters established by the Supreme Court. George Wallace, the Democratic governor of Alabama in the early 1960s, famously defied the Supreme Court's decision to desegregate American school via *Brown v. Board of Education* (1954). These informal displays of power restrict or weaken the powers of the Supreme Court.

Legislation Impacting Court Jurisdiction
Congress can enact legislation that may limit the Supreme Court's power by changing or modifying its jurisdictions.

Examples of Tasks Performed by Departments, Agencies, Commissions, and Government Corporations

Writing and Enforcing Regulations, Issuing Fines, and Testifying Before Congress
The various departments, agencies, commissions, and government corporations functioning within the United States government have the power write/enforce regulations, issue fines, and testify before Congress. These compliance monitoring tasks help ensure that the United States is running a safe and ethical government for its citizens. The Environmental Protection Agency (EPA), for example, is responsible for writing and enforcing pollution emissions regulation standards for big businesses. If these businesses violate the regulations, then they will be fined by the EPA on behalf of the United States government. If a big business egregiously violates regulations, placing the American government or its citizenry at risk, the EPA might force that company to testify before Congress.

Issue Networks and Iron Triangles
Iron triangles refers to the tripartite alliances, coalitions, or interest groups created by three dominant political influencers—bureaucracies, interest groups, and Congress (specifically congressional subcommittees)—to advocate for common initiatives, causes, acts, or laws. For instance, these three political influencers might join together to issue new initiatives or legislation focusing on reform efforts for industry, immigration, healthcare, or national security. Sometimes referred to as "subgovernments," these iron triangles can be viewed as nefarious entities that undermine democracy and equality. Likewise, they can also be used for the common good—it all depends on a person's perspective of the greater cause.

Two examples of iron triangle diagrams are offered below. Notice how quickly the support, lobbying, and financial contributions can potentially evolve into a nefarious consolidation of legislative power and financial gain.

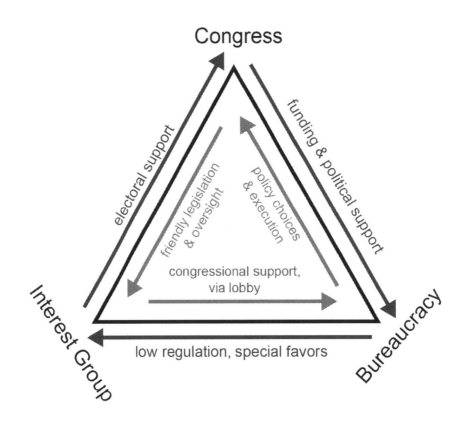

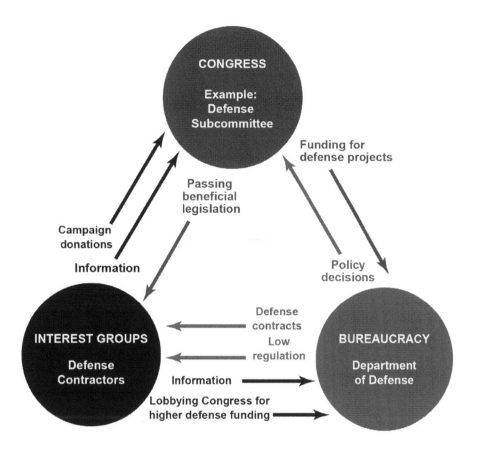

Issue networks are multi-pronged, multilateral relationships established by political alliances, coalitions, or interest groups in order to promote a particular policy, agenda, or platform. Issue networks tend to be more complex than iron triangles because they involve more stakeholders and, therefore, are built upon the foundations of more complicated, interconnected relationships. Issue networks can revolve around such agendas as gun rights, gun laws, capital punishment, universal healthcare, or abortion. These issue networks can be multipartisan or partisan in nature, meaning they can either draw from multiple political parties or garner their support from one political party.

Below is an example diagram that tries to convey the complexities of issue networks. Notice it attempts to illustrate just how "messy" these networks can be in comparison to iron triangles.

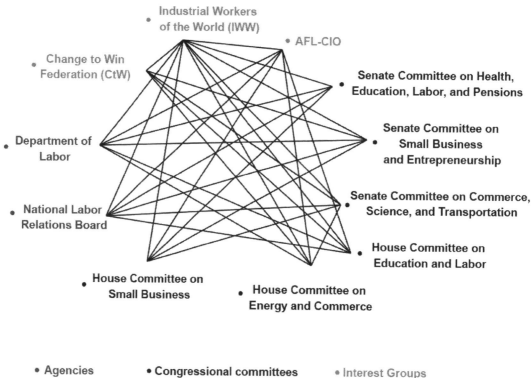

Minimum Wage Policy

Major Similarities and Differences between Iron Triangles and Issue Networks		
Iron Triangle (Unique Characteristics)	Similarities Between Iron Triangles and Issue Networks	Issue Networks (Unique Characteristics)
Exist independently of one another Difficult, but not impossible, to dismantle Mutually dependent and tripartite Some scholars believe they are being replaced by issue networks	Both marry governmental and extra-governmental affairs	Relationship(s) between bureaucracies are not as rigid as iron triangles More complicated, multilateral networks (move beyond the tripartite iron triangle model) Consist of a wider range of people

The Impact of Political Patronage on the Effectiveness of the Bureaucracy

Patronage refers to the act of hiring or appointing someone to a bureaucratic position based on their political affiliation or personal support rather than their individual merit. Often referred to as "the spoils system," patronage-based bureaucracies tend to lower the professionalism, specialization, and neutrality of government organizations. A civil service based bureaucracy creates permanent branches of governmental administration that hire and promote employees based on merit (i.e., skill and hard work). Merit-based bureaucracies tend to strengthen the professionalism, specialization, and neutrality of government organizations.

Discretionary and Rule-Making Authority to Implement Policy

Through executive appointment, the following departments, agencies, and commissions are granted discretionary and rule-making authority to implement policy:

- **Department of Homeland Security:** Formed in 2002, in the year following the September 11 attacks on New York City and Washington, D.C., the Department of Homeland Security is a bureaucratic department of the U.S. federal government tasked with protecting U.S. citizens by implementing presidentially-backed initiatives and processes for anti-terrorism, transportation security, border control, disaster prevention and crisis control, immigration and customs, and cybersecurity.

- **Department of Transportation:** Formed in 1967, as the U.S. federal highway system began to expand in the Cold War era, the Department of Transportation is a bureaucratic department of the U.S. federal government tasked with protecting the U.S. highways, airways, and railways, overseeing the management and creation of all three modes of transportation.

- **Department of Veterans Affairs:** Formed in 1930 in response to the growing need to consolidate federal support for military veterans from the World War I era, the Department of

Veterans Affairs is a Cabinet-level agency of the U.S. federal government tasked with providing comprehensive benefits to veterans, including home loans, educational assistance, life insurance, disability compensation, and burial and memorial support.

- **Department of Education:** Formed in 1979, under the reform-minded leadership of President Jimmy Carter, the Department of Education is a Cabinet-level agency of the U.S. federal government tasked with overseeing the collection of data and dispersal of federal aid to public schools. Following the passage of the No Child Left Behind (NCLB) Act, the role of this Cabinet-level agency has expanded dramatically to include ensuring the quality of public school standards and curricula through the monitoring of various accountability structures.

- **Environmental Protection Agency (EPA):** Formed in 1970, following the congressional ratification of an executive order signed by President Richard Nixon, the EPA is an independent agency within the U.S. federal government tasked with creating and enforcing a variety of regulations that ensure and promote human health and environmental protection/safety.

- **Federal Elections Commission (FEC):** Formed in 1974, through amendments made to the Federal Election Campaign Act of 1971, the FEC is an independent U.S. federal regulatory agency tasked with creating and monitoring regulatory laws that ensure campaign financing— particularly with regard to the public funding of presidential elections—stays true to a certain set of parameters and prohibitions.

- **Securities and Exchange Commission (SEC):** Formed in 1934, in the midst of the Great Depression, the SEC is an independent U.S. federal regulatory agency tasked with regulating the securities industry and protecting the stock exchange from fraudulent efforts.

Methods Congress Uses to Ensure Legislation is Implemented Properly

Committee Hearings
Sometimes referred to as the Elastic Clause, the Sweeping Clause, or the Necessary and Proper Clause, the final Clause of Article I, Section 8 of the U.S. Constitution affords Congress with the power "[t]o make all laws which shall be necessary and proper for carrying into execution" all federal powers afforded by the U.S. Constitution. This clause legitimizes all motives and methods for Congressional oversight, including committee hearings and "power of the purse." The Elastic Clause has historically allowed Congress to maintain broad oversight through a set of committees, or agencies, that can hold various committee hearings to review legislation, oversee executive issues or activities, investigate scandals or suspicious behaviors, confirm (or deny) presidential appointments, ratify treaties, and review polices outside of Washington, D.C.

Overall, there are four types of committee hearings, as defined in the table below:

Type of Committee Hearing	Definition
Legislative Hearings	Legislative hearings gather more information about a particular piece of legislation with a subject matter that is worth further investigation. Legislative hearings are sometimes carried out prior to the introduction of a bill in order to further (re)shape the forthcoming legislation.
Oversight Hearings	Oversight hearings can be used to review and monitor the executive branch to ensure that public policy is being implemented with fidelity.
Investigative Hearings	Investigative hearings are carried out when public officials allegedly commit unethical or criminal acts while in office. These hearings tend to be more confrontational than other types of committees.
Confirmation Hearings	While Article II of the U.S. Constitution grants the president the power to appoint executive and judicial officials at the federal level, the Senate must hold confirmation hearings to "advise and consent" to the president's decisions.

Power of the Purse:

The phrase **"power of the purse"** is used to describe a situation in government or politics in which one entity, branch, or department maintains the right to manipulate or control the efficacy of another entity, branch, or department by either withholding funding or creating strictures for the collection, disbursement, and/or use of funding (such as a federal budget, taxes, or foreign aid). Two portions of the U.S. Constitution declare that the "power of the purse" is vested in Congress: Article I, Section 9, Clause 7 and Article I, Section 8, Clause 1. The first portion declares that money cannot be withdrawn from the Treasury without congressional approval. Likewise, the budget has to be made by Congress's influence, according to this portion of the U.S. Constitution. The second portion of dictates that only Congress has the power to "collect taxes, duties, imposts, and excises." Additionally, this "power of the purse" is supposed to only be done in order "pay the debts and provide for the common defense and general welfare of the United States."

Congressional Oversight Provides a Check for Executive Power

Throughout the history of the United States government, the Elastic Clause, the Sweeping Clause, or the Necessary and Proper Clause has been invoked by Congress in order to curtail presidential power and check executive authorization and appropriation. This has especially been true in a post-World War II era (the mid-late twentieth century and early twenty-first century) in which presidential power has expanded rapidly. For instance, Congress invoked its "power of the purse" in order to limit executive/presidential power. In the twentieth and twenty-first centuries, Congress utilized its "power of the purse" to decrease military funding for U.S. conflicts and foreign aid for international military affairs. For instance, Congress's "power of the purse" was invoked to end military conflicts in Vietnam (1970s), Lebanon (1980s), and Nicaragua (1980s). It has also been used to re-appropriate funds for the War in Iraq (2000s).

The Impact of Presidential Ideology, Authority, and Influence on the Goals of the Administration

The "presidency" consists not only of the presidency, but of the entire complex executive branch that embodies the president's ideology, authority, and influence, as well. Presidents have historically used executive appointments and agencies to ensure that their ideology, authority, and influence is manifested in the commanding branch of government. The president's Cabinet and White House staffers, in particular, are usually strategically appointed to ensure that the president's ideology, whether conservative or liberal or moderate, pervades the executive branch. For instance, a more liberal president could use the Environmental Protection Agency to expand conservation efforts. Likewise, a more conservative president might use the same office to deregulate environmental restrictions.

Compliance Monitoring

Compliance monitoring occurs when executive agencies, such as the Environmental Protection Agency, or other governmental entities carry out audits and inspections, check permits and certifications, and produce/require reports to ensure that local government bodies and businesses are following federal regulations. Compliance monitoring can pose a challenge to policy implementation when the policies being implemented conflict with federal regulations. Compliance monitoring also notoriously slows down the process of implementing legislation due to the variety of intensive fidelity checks. An executive order that mandates the construction of an international pipeline, for instance, might conflict with the waste management regulations, conservations, and natural resource limitations established by the EPA.

Maintaining Bureaucracy's Accountability

The formal and informal powers of Congress can enact legislation that limits and oversees the responsibilities of the federal bureaucracy and its agencies. Using its power of the purse, Congress can also expand or cut the budgets of the agencies within the federal bureaucracy. In times of conflict, confusion, or alleged wrongdoing, Congress can carry out hearings to ensure that the federal bureaucracy and its agencies are making ethical and appropriate decisions. The president has the power to formally appoint members to the federal bureaucracy and its agencies; through these appointments, the president can informally influence the decisions of these leaders through political persuasion or pressure. The courts have the power to formally decide whether or not certain actions of the federal bureaucracy and its agencies can be deemed constitutional. Likewise, any other Supreme Court decisions can indirectly influence bureaucratic functions.

Practice Questions

Please use the graphic below to answer Questions 1 and 2:

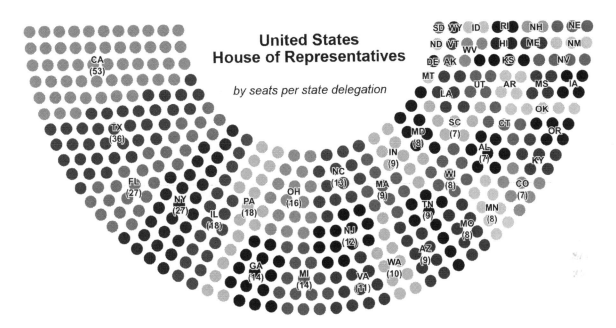

1. Which of the following statements is reflected in the graphic?

   a. The ten least-populated states possess a greater collective representation than the two most-populated states.

   b. The two most-populated states possess a greater collective representation than the ten least-populated states.

   c. The two most-populated states and ten least-populated states possess an equal number of representation.

   d. The ten most-populated states and two least-populated states possess an equal number of representatives.

2. Which of the following states would have the most votes within the Electoral College?

   a. Ohio

   b. Iowa

   c. Michigan

   d. South Dakota

Please use the map below to answer Questions 3 and 4:

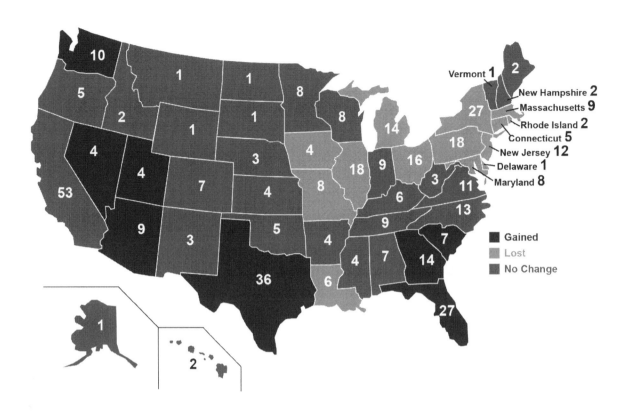

3. How many total electoral votes are accounted for by the states that gained representatives as a result of the 2010 U.S. census?

    a. 123

    b. 111

    c. 97

    d. 88

4. Which of the following statements is reflected in the map?

    a. More states gained or lost representatives than experienced no change at all.

    b. Most states that gained representatives were concentrated in the Pacific Northwest and Great Plains regions.

    c. Most states that lost representatives were concentrated in the Midwest and Northeast.

    d. More least-populous states lost representatives than more-populous states.

5. When are confirmation hearings carried out?

    a. When there is a need to review and monitor the executive branch to ensure that public policy is being implemented with fidelity

    b. Prior to the introduction of a bill in order to further (re)shape the forthcoming legislation

    c. When the president has appointed executive and judicial officials at the federal level

    d. When public officials allegedly commit unethical or criminal acts while in office

6. Which of the following is true regarding *stare decisis*?
    a. It is a mandatory practice for both the Supreme Court and lower courts.
    b. It allows courts to review past judicial decisions in order to inform their own judicial decision.
    c. It permits the Supreme Court to change past precedents through new judicial decisions.
    d. It is a rule that must be followed by lower courts only.

7. Which of the following is NOT a formal power of the presidency, but considered an informal power?
    a. Suspending Habeas Corpus during wartime
    b. Vetoing bills
    c. Appointing Cabinet members, ambassadors, consuls, Supreme Court judges, White House staff, and public ministers
    d. Acting as military "Commander in Chief"

8. Which of the following is an accurate comparison of the two court cases?

	Baker v. Carr (1961)	*Shaw v. Reno (1993)*
a.	Declared redistricting unconstitutional	Recognized the constitutional validity of unequal constituencies
b.	Legitimized the "one person, one vote" doctrine	Decided that racial gerrymandering was unconstitutional
c.	Decided that racial segregation within districts was unconstitutional	Opened the door to equal protection challenges
d.	Introduced popular vote for senators	Ended racial segregation within public schools

9. Within the upper chamber of Congress, who is responsible for counting majority votes?
    a. Speaker of the House
    b. Speaker pro tem
    c. Majority Leader
    d. Majority Whip

10. Which governing body is known to have the "power of the purse" within the U.S. government?
    a. Supreme Court
    b. Department of Commerce
    c. Congress
    d. Department of Labor

Please read the passage below and use it to answer Questions 11 and 12:

> The idea of a council to the Executive, which has so generally obtained in the State constitutions, has been derived from that maxim of republican jealousy which considers power as safer in the hands of a number of men than of a single man. If the maxim should be admitted to be applicable to the case, I should contend that the advantage on that side would not counterbalance the numerous disadvantages on the opposite side. But I do not think the rule at all applicable to the executive power. I clearly concur in opinion, in this particular, with a writer whom the celebrated Junius pronounces to be "deep, solid, and ingenious," that "the executive power is more easily confined when it is ONE;" that it is far more safe there should be a single object for the jealousy and watchfulness of the people; and, in a word, that all multiplication of the Executive is rather dangerous than friendly to liberty.

- Alexander Hamilton, *Federalist No. 70*

11. Which of the following ideological perspectives is MOST consistent with the passage?
    a. Republican
    b. Liberal
    c. Federalist
    d. Anti-Federalist

12. Which of the following statements is MOST consistent with the author's argument in the passage?
    a. Republican values dictate that it is in the best interest of the U.S. government to multiply executive power by electing multiple leaders to executive office.
    b. A single president would result in a single object of jealousy and watchfulness, which would ultimately threaten liberty through dictatorship.
    c. The multiplication of the executive office would be more of a threat to liberty than the election of single executive leader.
    d. The power of the executive office should be invested in state governments and constitutions, which would help balance executive power in the American Republic.

13. Which of the following actions is considered an implied power of the presidency rather than an explicit power?
    a. Treaty signings
    b. Vetoes
    c. Pocket vetoes
    d. Executive orders

Answer Explanations

1. B: The two most-populous states (California and Texas) possess a greater collective representation (eighty-nine representatives) than the ten least-populous states. All other answer choices do not reflect accurate comparisons of representation.

2. A: Ohio would have the most votes (sixteen) compared to Iowa (four), Michigan (fourteen), and South Dakota (one).

3. B: If you add up the representatives in states that gained representation, the total is 111. All other answer choices are incorrect.

4. C: Most states that lost representatives are located in the Rust Belt—the Midwest and Northeast—as illustrated by the light grey states on the map. Choice *B* is incorrect because most states that gained representation were scattered in the South and the West, not the Pacific Northwest and Great Plains. Choice *A* is incorrect because more states remained unchanged than lost or grained representation.

5. C: Under Article II of the U.S. Constitution, the president is granted the power to appoint executive and judicial officials at the federal level. As a "check," the Senate must hold confirmation hearings to "advise and consent" to the president's decisions. Choice *A* refers to oversight hearings, Choice *B* refers to legislative hearings, and Choice *D* refers to investigative hearings.

6. B: *Stare Decisis* is a Latin phrase that means "to stand by things decided." It allows courts to review past judicial decisions, particularly those made by the Supreme Court, in order to inform their own judicial decisions. Choice *A* is incorrect because *stare decisis* is not a mandatory practice, but rather a best practice in judicial decision making. Likewise, Choice *D* is incorrect, again because it is a principle, and not a rule. While the concept in Choice *C* itself is true—that the Supreme Court can change past precedents through new judicial decisions—*stare decisis* itself does not grant this authority.

7. A: While suspending Habeas Corpus during wartime is not a formal power of the U.S. president, as stated by the U.S. Constitution, it is an informal power. For example, President Abraham Lincoln employed this extraconstitutional tactic to protect the nation during the Civil War.

8. B: *Baker v. Carr* (1961) established the "one person, one vote" doctrine and *Shaw v. Reno* (1993) made it unconstitutional to redistrict according to racially-based gerrymandering standards. All other answer options do not reflect the decisions of these court cases.

9. D: The Majority Whip assists the Senate President and Majority Leader by counting votes. The Speaker of the House and the Speaker pro tem work in the lower chamber of Congress (the House of Representatives), not the upper chamber of Congress (the Senate).

10. C: Article I, Section 8 of the U.S. Constitution grants Congress with the "power of the purse," which is the power to coin money and create a federal budget. All other governmental agencies must follow Congress's budget, including the Department of Labor and the Department of Commerce. The Supreme Court can deem the budget to be unconstitutional only if it violates constitutional law.

11. C: *Federalist No. 70* is a quintessential Federalist (not Anti-Federalist) document because it openly attacks Republic and Anti-Federalist values that uphold the importance of states' rights over federal rights. It argues that a strong government is best reflected in strong federal leadership with one executive power instead of multiple state powers.

12. C: Again, Hamilton, the foremost federalist authority in the Early Republic, argued that a strong government is best reflected in strong federal leadership with one executive power instead of multiple state powers. He believed multiplying executive power is a threat to liberty. While a single executive is imperfect, and may be the target of resentment from citizens, it is the best option, according to the source. Choice *A* is incorrect because the document actually attacks classical republican values. Choice *B* is incorrect because Hamilton saw a single executive as a source of dissatisfaction, but not a major threat to liberty. Choice *D* is incorrect because its language, which is not reflected in the document, actually conveys Anti-Federalist sentiments.

13. D: Executive orders are examples of the president's informal powers because they are not explicitly established as a responsibility of the president within the U.S. Constitution. All other answer options are explicitly granted as presidential powers by the U.S. Constitution.

Unit 3: Civil Liberties and Civil Rights

Liberty and Order

The Bill of Rights

The Framers of the new **U.S. Constitution** felt necessary to establish the rights of the citizens of the new nation before all else in government. While the Constitution was certainly about the new structure of government, it was also more of a compact between the government and its people. To ensure that agreement, the people needed guaranteed rights apart from the government that would not, under any circumstance, be infringed upon.

What the Framers came up with is the first, and most important, section of the Constitution that would become known as the **Bill of Rights**. This groundbreaking agreement was a firm passage of rights from a government down to its citizens and established certain unalienable rights. Among them, the new Bill of Rights established a plethora of rights to property, speech, and opinions that would become the basis for many of the presently known basic rights of humans that much of the free world believes in today. Especially for its time, this was a new high for individual rights of citizens.

Civil Liberties

Of the aspects of the new Bill of Rights, the main grants to the electorate were the idea of **civil liberties**. Simply put, the idea of civil liberties is that there are certain rights that the populace should have that the government should not infringe upon. These are the rights of citizens to have the government not interfere in their lives. They are protected by the ten amendments within the Bill of Rights, and also include the rights that have been established by legal precedent throughout history, such as marriage rights.

The idea of civil liberty is the basis of the type of government-citizen relationship that the Framers so vehemently argued in favor of and, in some cases, fought for. The Framers believed that a person's opinion, speech, and property were necessary for a truly free people and a real and successful democratic government.

Court-Interpretation of the Bill of Rights

The Supreme Court has tangled over the interpretation and application of the Bill of Rights. Namely, the Court has seen struggles between state and federal application. The Court has almost universally found that, even in states where certain rights in the Bill of Rights are not guaranteed under that particular state constitution, the Bill of Rights applies to all people inside of each state in the United States.

This process is subject to the idea of **selective incorporation**, a doctrine the holds that states, whether willfully or not, are required to follow the Bill of Rights. In other words, no matter what a state constitution says, the Bill of Rights is part of its doctrine and any piece of the Bill of Rights that is missing from the state constitution is included, whether appearing in the text or not. When squabbles within the state bring the question of constitutionally of a given law pertaining to the Bill of Rights, the Supreme Court is the decider.

Components of the Bill of Rights

The Bill of Rights as a document is the first ten Amendments to the US Constitution. These amendments are divided up into groups that go hand-in-hand about what particular pieces of society and government they cover.

The first four amendments that are grouped together protect what is called the **individual liberties** of the citizens. Individual liberties are the peoples' constitutionally guaranteed rights and freedoms that are protected by law.

The **First Amendment** is probably the most well-known of the Bill of Rights: the freedom of religion, speech, press, assembly, and to petition. This amendment gives the universal rights of the people to be individuals and question and protest the government and its leaders.

The **Second Amendment** is the right to bear arms. This amendment gives a citizen the right to have a gun on their person and in their home.

The **Third Amendment** is a byproduct of the effects of the American Revolution: the right to not house soldiers during times of war. This was a reaction to the British idea of "quartering," where soldiers would enter a home and had to be provided for by the owners of the home for as long as the soldiers wanted.

The **Fourth Amendment**, the last of the individual liberties amendments, is the right to be protected from unreasonable search and seizure. This is the idea that the government doesn't have the power to take a citizen's property or search it for no reason. These amendments protect the right of the citizen broadly and their more direct protections of Locke's "life, liberty, and property."

The next four amendments are the protections regarding crimes and rights during a trial and arrest. These amendments guarantee a person's ability to defend themselves and have confidence that the government can't harass someone in court.

The **Fifth Amendment** guarantees due process and the right of protection from self-incrimination. It also sets the precedent that a person cannot be tried for major crimes with a grand jury indictment. This amendment guarantees an actual trial and system, as well as the popular "Plead the Fifth" option to avoid providing testimony that could damage oneself.

The **Sixth Amendment** is the right to a speedy trial, guaranteeing the government can't delay and drag cases out. It also guarantees an attorney and the right to confront witnesses, as well as an impartial jury.

The **Seventh Amendment** is the right to a jury trial in civil cases.

The **Eight Amendment** is the right to not be forced into excessive bail, fines, or cruel and unusual punishment. This protects people while they are going through the court system and makes sure that someone cannot be taken advantage of by the courts.

The final two amendments of the Bill of Rights are a response to arguments certain Framers had against including the Bill of Rights at all. Basically, people opposing the Bill of Rights believed that, by writing the rights down, anything they might miss would mean that it was not protected.

To quell those fears, the Framers included the **Ninth Amendment**, which says that there are other basic rights that are protected, even if they are not listed in the Bill of Rights. Basically, the Ninth Amendment says that there is more in the Bill of Rights that can't be listed, and that just because such rights are not written does not mean they aren't protected.

The **Tenth Amendment** takes this a step further, saying that any rights not listed in the Constitution are then designated to the federal government, after which the power falls to the states or to the people. This means that the federal government may only exercise the powers granted to it in the Constitution.

Going forward, we will take a deeper dive into these amendments and what they mean for us in the United States today.

The First Amendment

The First Amendment to the Constitution is widely considered the most important and easily the most memorable to most Americans. To more wholly understand pieces of the uber-important First Amendment, let's look at two key pieces. The first is the **establishment clause**. This states that "Congress shall make no law respecting the establishment of religion." This guarantees the separation of church and state.

This particular piece of the amendment has been challenged in court on a number of occasions, most famously in *Engel v. Vitale*. The case, considered by many to be a defining moment for the establishment clause, came about in the early 1960s and was centered around prayer in school.

The state of New York told teachers to lead students in prayer each morning before school. Parents unsupportive of this, including Steven Engle, sued the school district that had most recently adopted prayer on the grounds of violation of the establishment clause.

The court ruled that prayer violated the clause, arguing that by advocating for the prayer, the state of New York had supported religion. This is unconstitutional, the court argued, saying that it is strictly prohibited in the establishment clause.

The other key case centered around the establishment clause is the *Lemon v. Kurtzman* case that established the "Lemon test," which stated that laws are constitutional only if they have a secular purpose, don't advance or inhibit religion, and do not result in "excessive government entanglement" with religion.

Another key clause of the First Amendment is the **free exercise** clause. This clause, also centered around religion, states that Congress may not pass a law "prohibiting the free exercise of religion." Closely tied to the establishment clause, this piece of the First Amendment also has been the subject of court battles. Specifically, the case of *Wisconsin v. Yoder*.

This case centered around three Amish families in the early 1970s. The state of Wisconsin had a law requiring students to attend school until 16. The families, unwilling to send their children to school past the eighth grade, were subjected to fines from the state. The Amish believed that education, at least beyond the basic, was a threat to their way of life, and therefore did not support the children continuing their education by the state's standard.

The court ruled that the case did violate the free exercise clause. They argued that the Amish families—an established community in the United States—were free to exercise their religion and that their practice of it and belief outweighed the state's claim to want to educate the general populace to a higher standard. This propped up the free exercise clause as another strong defender of religious liberty independent of governmental interference.

The First Amendment Protects Symbolic Speech

Another key aspect of the First Amendment is the idea of free speech. While the idea of "speech" may sound pretty cut and dried, the Supreme Court has added some variants to the idea of what constitutes "speech" in the United States. One of these famous cases is the *Tinker v. Des Moines Independent Community School District* case of 1969.

In Tinker, three Iowa teens decided to protest the ongoing Vietnam War at school by wearing black armbands. This protest, while silent, prompted the school to suspend the students, as well as announce that students who wore the armbands had to stop wearing them or would be suspended. The three students refused the order and were suspended.

Their parents sued the school district, with the Supreme Court hearing the case a few years later. The Court found that the school district had violated the students' right to freedom of speech and expression. The Court stated that the students had a right to "symbolic" speech, and that by wearing the armbands, they were making a statement. This type of speech is protected the same way as regular speech and therefore the school had no right to prevent it.

The decision reaffirmed the Supreme Court's commitment to protection of speech, even adding a new wrinkle to what constitutes as speech under the First Amendment. Symbolic speech has come to encompass many differing kinds of speech over the years, from signs to public protests and flag burning.

Interpretations of the First Amendment that Limit Speech

While in most cases, absolute free speech is the model goal of the Framers and most of the United States, there have been cases that have set some parameters around what is and isn't protected speech. Since the drafting of the First Amendment, there have been many cases and situations that have been looked at when certain speeches are protected, with mixed results.

Time, Place, and Manner Restrictions
The first is the **time, place, and manner restrictions.** These restrictions are used by the court to state that there are some restrictions to speech the government can place if there are certain impediments that may come from said speech. An example is that some cities may require permits for larger protests or demonstrations just due to traffic or disruption of businesses. This isn't seen as limiting speech so much as keeping things moving.

Defamatory, Offensive, and Obscene Statements and Gestures
There are also some forms of speech that the government can penalize in certain situations. The first of these is **defamatory speech**. This is any speech that uses false statements or ideas to damage a person's reputation. There are two forms, depending on the medium: it is called **libel** when it occurs in print, while defamatory speech that is in spoken word is called **slander**.

Beyond this is **offensive** or **obscene speech**. The Supreme Court has struggled to give a clear definition of this, but over time, it has come to mean lewd or sexual media. It's been defined by the Court as applying to media that "to the average person applying contemporary community standards" can show offensive content and lack any artistic merit.

"Clear and Present Danger" Speech
A popular case that provided a defining limitation on the First Amendment is *Schenck v. United States*. This case centered around the **Espionage Act**, a law passed by Congress that made the effort to curb

criticism of the war effort during World War I. Activists Charles Schenck and Elizabeth Baer mailed fliers urging people to disregard calls to the draft through peaceful protest. They were arrested and convicted, and then appealed saying the Espionage Act violated the First Amendment.

The Court found that the protest was not protected as free speech. The Court famously held that speech creating "clear and present danger" was not protected as free speech. While later overturned, this "clear and present danger" test would be the first true measure of the Court to curb the free speech part of the First Amendment and would keep the Espionage Act floating through the Vietnam War.

New York Times Co. Versus United States

Not all cases before the Supreme Court walked back First Amendment protections, however. In the early 1970s, the United States was digging deeper into hostile actions in Vietnam. In 1971, the *New York Times* obtained leaked materials from within the Pentagon that detailed the lies that the federal government had pushed about war efforts in Vietnam. They published the first chapter in 1971, and the Nixon White House filed injunctions to prevent the rest from being released. The Supreme Court took the case soon after, it was known as **New York Times Co. v. United States.**

The Court was looking at the issue of **prior restraint**, a term used when the government looks to block something before release, where otherwise the government would seek legal damages or judgment after release. The Court established heavy precedent in their ruling for the *New York Times*, saying that the "First Amendment supports the view that the press must be left free to publish news, whatever the source, without censorship, injunctions, or prior restraints." Further, the Court found that the Nixon Administration had not met the "heavy burden of showing justification" for prior restraint. They found that military operations would not be affected, as this was a history of actions.

This ruling established heavy justifications for prior restraint and showed that the Court would challenge governmental press censorship, even in the face of national security concerns. The ruling was a direct contrast to the **Schenck v. United States** case and gave strong protections to the press.

The Supreme Court's Decisions on the Second Amendment

Easily one of the most controversial of the amendments, the Second Amendment is the ever-debated "right to bear arms." It is fully quoted as: "A well-regulated militia being necessary to the security of a free state and the right of the people to keep and bear arms shall not be infringed."

This particular amendment has been the subject of much debate, especially since the end of the 1960s. Congress has seen much debate over laws on restrictions of this amendment and has gone back and forth on regulations. The Supreme Court has also been busy with this amendment and has provided some insight to their thinking when it comes to gun ownership by individuals.

Members of the Court have ruled systematically that they value individual liberty over all when debating this amendment. They have found that there are pure protections for gun owners, even in today's world, and that the amendment must be allowed to stay. In two notable decisions in the past decade that involved restrictions on gun ownership in different states, the Court has ruled that gun control regulations in those cases gave the government too much power and upheld individual liberties of gun owners, showing the amendment will be protected at a heavy bar like the others.

The Eighth Amendment and "Cruel and Unusual Punishment"

The Eighth Amendment of the Constitution is centered on protections from the court system imposed by the government. Specifically, it provides protection from excessive fines, bail, and inflicting "cruel and unusual punishment." While the first two pieces of the amendment are straightforward, the phrase, "cruel and unusual," has seen many debates over time in the court system, primarily regarding the death penalty.

For most of the lifetime of the United States, the debates the Supreme Court heard about the Eighth Amendment have mostly been limited to prison conditions, bail, and fines. But over the past few decades, the attention has turned to one of the last remaining forms of corporal punishment: the death penalty.

While the Framers would never have envisioned a debate around this type of punishment, lethal injection in particular has seen much criticism. In certain cases, the way the lethal drugs are delivered can lead to a painful and lengthy death, especially if they aren't administered correctly. This has brought the argument that lethal injection is an inhumane way to execute, and that the states shouldn't be doing it at all.

The Supreme Court, however, has disagreed. While they have provided new protections against executing minors or mentally impaired individuals, the Court has been consistent in arguing that the death penalty is constitutional and doesn't yet fit the boundaries of cruel and unusual. However, as times change, it seems that the courts may find themselves wrapped up in this debate for a long time.

The Second and Fourth Amendments and Public Safety

The Second Amendment as originally written and sat mostly unchanged for the first two centuries of the United States. But, in more recent times, there have been a greater number of challenges in the courts and society in general to the ideas behind, and original intent of, the amendment. Guns have certainly changed in the last two hundred years and with rises in gun violence and killings, the debate over the Second Amendment has become mainstream.

In particular, the debate has centered around the line between individual freedom—in this case, the right to keep firearms—and public order and safety. An example of this balance was the Brady Bill, an act named after Ronald Reagan's aide who was shot during an assassination attempt on the former president. The Bill placed the first real restrictions on firearms and their purchase and was a source of real debate on the political spectrum.

Recently, however, the Supreme Court has stepped onto the side of personal freedom, ruling in cases like *DC v. Heller* and *McDonald v. Chicago* that certain gun control legislative acts are unconstitutional. The courts have rebuffed political actions that ban or inhibit gun purchases at both the state and federal level, defending the right of personal freedom in their purchase over the argued danger to public safety.

The Fourth Amendment's protections against unlawful search and seizure have seen similar debates in the last decade or so. As the world has gotten more digital and connected, the ability to stay on top of many different threats within society has gotten harder. After the terrorist attacks on 9/11, the federal government upped its effort to watch citizens with the creation of the National Security Agency. This agency, coupled with the work of the FBI and CIA, increased surveillance on citizens in an effort to combat possible terrorist activities.

The breadth of actions that the agencies employed didn't fully become public until 2013, when it was learned that the NSA was using phone and digital data from phone companies to spy on American citizens and foreign leaders. This brought on a heavy debate that continues today about the role of the government and whether the implied threat of terrorist attacks is enough justification for the government to spy without warrant or disclosure. Some people argue that it's an overreach and violation, with calls for complete transparency, while others argue that the federal government should take any action necessary to protect national security.

Selective Incorporation

While the Bill of Rights itself is seen to be the pact between the people governed and the federal government of rights that are protected, down at the state level, things can get a little murkier. For most of the nineteenth and twentieth century, the Bill of Rights and subsequent amendments have been left as standing alone and self-explanatory in their defense. However, states have challenged certain protections and argued in certain cases that those federal guidelines don't apply to their laws.

Enter the **Fourteenth Amendment**. Known for the section about "due process," the Fourteenth Amendment acts, in contrast to the Fifth Amendment's restriction on the federal government's powers, as a restriction on the states. Specifically, it states that certain rights are guaranteed over state law, including citizenship, due process, and equal protection. The due process clause has been used to rebuff state law that has encroached on certain parts of the Bill of Rights in recent years.

McDonald v. Chicago

McDonald v. Chicago is one of these cases. In this case, the city of Chicago, in an effort to put a dent in the growing violence within the city, implemented a handgun ban similar to that adopted by Washington D.C. The ban restricted gun ownership in the city and the ability to buy guns. Otis McDonald, a Chicago resident, filed suit against the city arguing that the ban was a direct violation of his Second Amendment right to bear arms. Once at the Supreme Court level, the Court began to unpack the case as one not centered on the Second Amendment, but rather, the Fourteenth Amendment.

Specifically, the justices looked at the privileges and immunities clause that argued that the state cannot restrict certain **fundamental rights** laid out in the language of the Fourteenth Amendment. These rights, outlined by the Supreme Court as "implicit in the concept of ordered liberty," are rights that are both protected against the federal and state government. Using this, the Supreme Court found that the Second Amendment is a fundamental right, and the ban on handguns would be a threat to ownership of a gun for defense in the home. Thus, they struck down the ban.

Different amendments have been applied to the state level using this clause in a process known as **incrementalism**. This way of application is a case-by-case application of rights of the Bill of Rights to the state. This is juxtaposed to the idea of **total incorporation**, a belief held by some justices that all rights in the Bill of Rights apply to the state without exception, but this practice has yet to be affirmed by the Supreme Court as a whole.

Rulings in Favor of States' Power to Restrict Individual Liberty

In most cases, the Supreme Court almost always uses its powers of review to affirm the rights of the individual over the government at both the state and federal level. However, there have been restrictions placed and there have been cases where the states have been granted power to restrict certain aspects of individual liberty for the common good. This has applied to various cases, most notably in the case of threat to public safety.

We've already discussed one of these types of limitations in the case of **Schenck v. United States**. This was one of the earliest examples of the Court arguing that speech was not unilaterally protected when it interfered with the public good. In this case, the students that protested the war were not guaranteed the protection of their speech, as the war effort was seen as having greater concern.

In addition, the freedom of speech protection in the Bill of Rights has been noted to not protect certain types of speech. Most notably, the Supreme Court has ruled that speech that results in "incitement" is not protected. Speech that could lead to violence or direct of violence is not free speech and can be limited. For example, if a person is speaking in a crowd and tells the crowd that someone must attack another person, the action would be called **incitement** and would not be protected.

These limitations are just a few examples of limitations that can be placed on the Bill of Rights, meaning that the rights are not always absolute. But more directly, the Supreme Court has allowed for states to limit other parts of the Bill of Rights when necessary to protect public safety.

The Miranda Rule

In general, the Fifth Amendment offers the protection of the right to remain silent—a way to protect against self-incrimination. The Sixth Amendment is the constitutional guarantee of a speedy and public trial. This is an important area of the law and has seen some clarification by the Supreme Court. These amendments were most notably defined in **Miranda v. Arizona**. In this case, a young man raped a young girl in Arizona. Police presented the girl a lineup of suspects, to which she said that she thought that Miranda was the one but couldn't be sure. They then went to Miranda and told him that she had said it was him, to which he then admitted to the crime and a few others.

The Court took this case and ruled that his admission was a violation of the Fifth Amendment, and therefore the confession was inadmissible. This ushered in the **Miranda Rights**. If you've ever watched police shows on television, the Miranda Rights are likely very familiar. The officer will tell the suspect that they have the right to remain silent and the right to an attorney. They will then ask if they consent to answer questions. If the answer is no, they must stop questioning. These protections changed the way confessions and police interactions with suspects would be going forward.

However, these protections can be averted if there is a threat to public safety. This exception is called the **public safety exception**. With this, officers can compel someone to speak in spite of their constitutional protection not to if there is a threat to public safety. An example of a situation that might require this is a terrorist attack, where police will interrogate to determine the location of other suspects or a potential bomb.

Pre-Trial Rights

The Sixth Amendment in large part was meant to serve as a safeguard against those accused of crimes. This amendment was a serious concern of the Framers, as there had been abuses under the British system with those accused being held and punished beyond a reasonable amount for almost any offense. The protections granted in the Bill of Rights made sure everyone had protection under the law.

The Right to Legal Counsel, a Speedy and Public Trial, and an Impartial Jury
The Sixth Amendment granted many pre-trial rights to the accused. First is the right to legal counsel, a safeguard that guarantees legal representation for everyone. Second is the right to a speedy and public trial. This was particularly pertinent in the Framers' arguments, as they sought to be sure that the government could not drag processes out indefinitely for investigation purposes.

Third is the right of an impartial jury. This protection guarantees those charged are granted a fair trial by their peers. Fourth is the right to be alerted of charges against you. And fifth is the right to confront accusers and other witnesses. This is a protection to prevent false accusations.

Protection Against Warrantless Searches of Cell Phone Data Under the Fourth Amendment

Other protections sought to limit the government's reach over citizens' rights in trial situations. The Fourth Amendment prevents the use of warrantless searches, preventing the government from simply coming after private citizens at any time and without any warning. This right in particular has become much more important lately, especially with the rise of cell phones and the Internet.

The Patriot and USA Freedom Acts

As touched on briefly before, cell phone and internet metadata has been of state concern since the turn of the century. Following the 9/11 terrorist attacks, Congress passed the **Patriot Act**, a law that allowed the counterintelligence agencies (FBI, CIA, and NSA) to collect almost any data that wanted to assist in national security protection. The breadth of this system was discovered when Edward Snowden leaked information about the NSA's massive data collection.

Many disputed the collections as a violation of the Fourth Amendment, and the Supreme Court saw many cases that way as well. Public pressure pushed many to admonish the Patriot Act, but the leaks only began nearly ten years after the law was passed. When the Patriot Act expired in 2015, Congress replaced it with the **USA Freedom Act**. This act restored some of the capabilities of the agencies to collect data, but instead of collecting it widely and broadly, Congress limited the capabilities to only asking companies for the data of specific people. To get that data, the government has to show there was a connection between the individual and a foreign power or terrorist group.

While still not seen by many as abiding by the Fourth Amendment protections, the new law certainly is a better step toward personal freedom than the Patriot Act.

Implications of the Due Process Clause

The Sixth Amendment's protections have long stood at the federal level, but these protections haven't always been applied to the states. As we have seen, the due process clause has only been used to apply basic protections back down to the states in recent years.

Gideon v. Wainwright

A prominent case that applied more of the Bill of Rights to the state is the famous case of *Gideon v. Wainwright*. The landmark case came after a court in Florida refused to provide Clarence Gideon a lawyer. Gideon, who was accused of robbery, had no funds to provide his own counsel and was not educated. In the ensuing case, the state convicted Gideon and sentenced him to five years. While in prison, Gideon educated himself on the Constitution and eventually found that the Fourteenth Amendment's due process clause made the Sixth Amendment's right to legal counsel apply to the state. He then filed an appeal, which the Florida Supreme Court found against him. Gideon then turned to the Supreme Court, who took up his case in 1963.

In the case, Gideon's lawyer argued that a prominent lawyer named Clarence Darrow, then regarded as one of the greatest criminal lawyers in history, had at one time hired a lawyer to defend himself. If even Darrow needed a lawyer, they argued, then certainly someone not educated in the law would absolutely require one. The Supreme Court saw it this way too, ruling that the due process clause extended the protections of the Sixth Amendment to the state. The case was retried, and Gideon was acquitted after the trial.

<u>The Exclusionary Rule</u>

Another important decision that granted further rights to state citizens was the case of **Mapp v. Ohio**. In this case, police in Ohio raided the home of Dollree Mapp, suspecting her of harboring a suspect in a bombing case. They did not have a warrant but entered the home anyway. While they did not find the suspect, they did find a trunk containing pornographic materials. Mapp was arrested for violating an Ohio law outlawing possession of pornography. The court found Mapp guilty.

Mapp then appealed the case to the Supreme Court. The following decision resulted in the **exclusionary rule**, a mandate that any evidence found in an illegal search and seizure cannot be used to charge someone with a crime. This reaffirmed the protection of the Fourth Amendment for states, as well as defined a new parameter for state police. Mapp was later acquitted of her charges.

The Right to Privacy and the Due Process Clause

Beginning in the early 1960s, the Supreme Court began to take up the issue of privacy. The Court expanded protections to the **right of privacy** in the Constitution. While not named as a right in the Constitution, the Court has ruled that privacy is a protected right in many cases. Specifically, the Court has stated that several of the amendments in the Bill of Rights create a "**penumbra**" of privacy. They've argued that, for example, the Fourth Amendment's protections against unreasonable searches grant a protection to the right of privacy.

<u>Roe v. Wade</u>

The biggest case that made the case of right of privacy is the ever-debated case of **Roe v. Wade**. The case revolved around Norma McCorvey, who went by the alias of Jane Roe in court proceedings. Roe wanted to have an abortion in her home state of Texas but found that the state didn't provide any facilities to have one done safely and legally. She petitioned the state and was denied, and the case went before the Supreme Court.

In the landmark ruling, the Supreme Court found that the state could not limit abortions by law, as the right to an abortion is protected in the purported protections of privacy that the Constitution implies. The Court did allow some limits to remain, primarily on the second and third trimesters of pregnancy, but did reinforce the right of women to have the procedure done.

These rights to privacy cases increased throughout the twentieth century and the debate around the issue has grown. Particularly in the follow-up of **Roe v. Wade**, there have been debates about discretion between the state and federal government over which statues constitute privacy and which do not.

Civic Participation in a Representative Democracy

Civil Rights

Since the Civil War, the idea of civil rights has been imbedded in American political debate. Starting in the 1960s, the Civil Rights Movement changed the way we talked about civil rights and brought the debate to the forefront of the American public. Legally, the debate centered on the Fourteenth Amendment. This amendment, civil rights activists argued, gave everyone guaranteed and unfettered protections under the law via the due process and equal protection clauses.

As the women's rights movement continued to move forward as well, there were again pushes for equal protection for all Americans. An example of this was the aforementioned **Roe v. Wade** decision. But beyond those protections, both women and minorities began to push back against a political and legal system that had long kept them from being a true part of the system.

From the "separate but equal" ruling in **Plessy v. Ferguson** that kept segregation legal throughout the early twentieth century to limitations on the rights of voting for both African-Americans and women, people were ready to change the system. In the minds of many of their leaders, there already was the change to the system within the Constitution: the Fourteenth Amendment. Going forward, civil and women's rights leaders would use this amendment to argue for their representation in a fight still lingering into today.

Examples of the Equal Protection Clause Supporting and Motivating Social Movements

Women's Rights Movement
Many movements began to spring to life in the 1960s and 1970s that pushed the Fourteenth Amendment's protections into the limelight of the political and legal world. The **women's rights movement** saw most of their movement begin following the release of a book titled *The Feminine Mystique* by Betty Friedan. The book cited issues with the place of women in society and became a calling card for change for women in the United States.

Following the outpouring of support, a group called the **National Organization of Women (NOW)** began to push the idea further into the mainstream. They pushed for the rights of women through changes to the legislation and challenged sex discrimination. Throughout much of the 1960s, the women's movement succeeded in advancing women's rights in the workforce, colleges, and voting with the Fourteenth Amendment's equal protection clause.

Letter from a Birmingham Jail
Elsewhere throughout the 1960s, the fight for civil rights was growing to a fever pitch. **Dr. Martin Luther King**, a pastor from Montgomery, Alabama, wrote what became the famous **Letter from a Birmingham Jail** following his arrest in 1963 for protesting segregation. The letter, written from his jail cell, was published throughout the United States. It argued that civil rights leaders should not wait for their cause and that "one has a moral responsibility to disobey unjust laws." He critiqued the idea of patience in the matter and called people to action in the fight for civil rights. Dr. King would become the preeminent leader for the Civil Rights Movement, giving the famous "I Have a Dream" speech that would spearhead the movement to the passage of the **Civil Rights Act of 1964**, prohibiting segregation or discrimination on the basis of race, color, sex, religion, or national origin.

The fight for civil rights was one that dominated most of the twentieth century. Many cases before the Supreme Court advanced the case for these rights. Among them is the historic case of **Brown v. Board of Education of Topeka,** which will be summarized in greater detail later. This case, argued by attorney **Thurgood Marshall**, desegregated schools and started the calls for ends of segregation throughout society. Marshall would later become the first African American Supreme Court justice.

The LGBTQ Movement
While those were the two most known movements from that time period, there were other movements started that continue today. One such is the **LGBTQ movement** that sought the equal protection for all lesbian, gay, bisexual, transsexual, and queer citizens in the United States. This movement, gaining traction in the 1970s, began arguing that the Fourteenth Amendment extended protections down to them as well and has seen heavy pushes all the way through today.

Another key movement starting around this time was the **pro-life movement**. This movement began in response to changes in the law surrounding the **Roe v. Wade** decision earlier in the 1950s. This group, led by the National Right to Life Committee, argued—and continues to argue—against abortion protections. They believe that the Fourteenth Amendment protections, rather than guaranteeing privacy as the Supreme Court found, actually give protections to infants in the womb, and that constitutional protections begin at conception.

Competing Policy-Making Interests

Governmental Responses to Social Movements

The federal government has had many different movements and strains against it over the course of the last two centuries. None have rocked the system quite like the Women's Rights Movement and the Civil Rights Movement. These two movements, originating during the same time period, challenged the status quo in a systematic and organic fashion. The new conflict needed decisive action, and as time pressed on, the federal government came through with ways to change a system resistant to change.

Brown v. Board of Education

The first shockwave was sent out through the courts. In the early 1950s, the Supreme Court was looking toward the issue of segregation. They had examined various cases on the matter, and the Court was beginning to look at the issue of "separate but equal," as the Supreme Court had ruled decades earlier, as being an issue in today's time. Their chance to do something about it came in the landmark case of **Brown v. Board of Education**.

This case, which began in Kansas, centered around an African American elementary school student who was made to attend a segregated school. Her father sought out legal representation to fight and found the NAACP and future Supreme Court Justice Thurgood Marshall. The case went before the Supreme Court later in 1954. In the landmark ruling, the Court ruled that "in the field of public education, separate but equal has no place." This ruling effectively ended segregation practices in a variety of places within the country and gave the impending Civil Rights Movement a massive boost.

The Civil Rights Act and the Voting Rights Act

However, the federal government can't just rely on the Supreme Court. The most effective method of change in society is through an act of Congress. As the Civil Rights Movement pushed forward, leaders like Martin Luther King Jr. championed the extension of the protections the Supreme Court established in **Brown v. Board of Education** into every aspect of life. In 1964, the movement got its wish: the **Civil Rights Act**, a sweeping legislative act that barred any discrimination on the basis of color, national origin, race, religion, or sex. The next year, Congress took things a step further with the **Voting Rights Act**. This legislation sought to tackle the last vestige of segregation in the South: voting. The Voting Rights Act made all discrimination in voting illegal, including Jim Crow era tactics like poll taxes, literary tests, and grandfather clauses designed to limit minority voting.

Title IX

Just a few years later, the Women's Rights Movement would get their big victory with the passage of **Title IX,** the sweeping legislation designed to limit the male domination of schools. The legislation targeted all schools getting federal funding and banned them from discriminating against female students in admissions, the classroom, and in sporting events. It massively expanded female access to schools and higher education.

Constitutionalism

Court Decisions Involving Minority Rights

While most of our learning about the Supreme Court has been their reversal of many decisions that have been consequential to the Union, the impact and decision making of the Supreme Court has been very indicative of the time period of their decisions. With almost every landmark decision, good and bad, there have been changes to the way the country operates legally and socially.

The "Separate But Equal" Doctrine
In the post-Civil War United States, the country desperately wanted to place stopgap protections against African Americans falling back into the same types of slavery conditions that they had been subjected to for nearly two centuries. Enter the Fourteenth Amendment and its equal protection clause, designed to extend the promises of the Bill of Rights all the way down to the states.

But in the late 1800s, states began to rebuff those mandates from the federal government. They began to institute Jim Crow laws, designed to relegate African Americans to second-class citizens. What would result was a systematic separation of white and black citizens: from schools to churches to trains. One particular case worsened this effect. In the case of **Plessy v. Ferguson**, the Supreme Court took up the issue of segregation and officially gave it the green light. In a landmark ruling, the Court found that segregation was fine as long as both options were equal. And as such, "separate but equal" was born.

Brown v. Board of Education
That ruling would cement segregation in the United States for almost sixty years, echoing the views of the nation at that time. But as times and opinions would change, so too would the Supreme Court's. This came to head with the ruling of **Brown v. Board of Education**. This ruling in 1954, as discussed previously, used the Fourteenth Amendment to bring the equal protection clause down to the state level. This ruling outlawed segregation, paving the way for the end of second-class treatment of African Americans. Following that ruling, more protections in the Civil Rights Act and Voting Rights Act followed nearly a decade later.

Redistricting
However, not all protections designed to limit unfair representation work out in the way one would think. At the end of the twentieth century, redistricting for voting became a hot button issue. **Redistricting** is the act of splitting up congressional maps in states to create voting districts. This process has become increasingly partisan as time has gone on.

In 1993, North Carolina was tasked with redistricting their map. Once submitted for review, the Attorney General took issue with the lack of representation for the black population in North Carolina, with only one district being black-majority. As a result, the proposed map was rejected. North Carolina then proposed a second map that created two majority-black districts, with one being abnormal in shape. Residents of North Carolina sued over the map, resulting in the case of **Shaw v. Reno**. In the case, the Supreme Court found the new map unconstitutional, arguing that while race must be kept in mind and the Voting Rights Act must be followed, the map must also be reasonable, and the second map violated the equal protection clause in the Fourteenth Amendment.

The Affirmative Action Debate

Race and equal protection of the law have been at the forefront of the national debate ever since the not-so-long-ago Civil Rights Movement. Even since the passing of the Civil Rights Act, the federal government has continued to debate additional improvements. Since its adoption, the federal government has made different attempts to try and bridge the gaps between white and black Americans in a variety of ways. One way that gained popularity in the government in the 1960s is **affirmative action**.

This designation for schools was seen as a way to fix the gap between white and black representation in higher learning institutions that never matched the population splits. Schools—especially colleges— were a majority white, especially colleges, and the federal government saw that the way to fix this issue was for schools to have quotas for a number of minority-represented students. This, predictably, has been the subject of much debate.

The Supreme Court has been equally divided on this issue. In 2003, the Court saw two of these cases that further muddied the issue. In *Grutter v. Bollinger*, the Court ruled that race could be a factor in admission processes, as long as it is just one factor. Also, they ruled that it is acceptable if the goal of the practice is to achieve a diverse student body. However, in *Gratz v. Bollinger*, the Court took a step back in a ruling that went against affirmative action if the system is a quota or points-based system.

These debates underline a disagreement on the belief of the **"colorblind" Constitution**, a point of view many hold that the Constitution protects all citizens, and that no extra laws are needed for protection for minorities. Proponents cite that there is no need for further protection when the Constitution is explicit in its protections of all.

Practice Questions

1. Which of these is NOT a protection within the Bill of Rights?
   a. Right to due process
   b. Freedom of speech
   c. Right to privacy
   d. Right to a speedy and fair trial

2. The establishment clause deals with which of the following?
   a. The relationship between government and labor unions
   b. The relationship between government officials and lobbyists
   c. The relationship between government and the creation of new federal courts
   d. The relationship between government and religion

3. The Supreme Court has ruled that the federal government may limit a certain type of speech without violation of the First Amendment. What is an example of that type of speech?
   a. Students wearing black arm bands to protest a war
   b. A person writes a newspaper article using falsified quotes to attack a rival's character
   c. A student giving a speech outside of Congress protesting the passing of a bill that cuts school funding
   d. A citizen writes up a flier about the dangers of the government's new hunting regulations and hangs them up all over town

4. The NSA's surveillance of Americans' phones and data was underlined as a violation of which amendment of the Bill of Rights?
   a. The Fourth Amendment's protection of unlawful search and seizure
   b. The Fifth Amendment's due process clause
   c. The Fifth Amendment's protection against self-incrimination
   d. The Eighth Amendment's protection against "cruel and unusual punishment"

5. What is the term used to describe the way the Supreme Court used the Fourteenth Amendment to apply the Bill of Rights down to the state level?
   a. Total incorporation
   b. Due process
   c. Fundamental rights
   d. Incrementalism

6. Which of these is NOT one of the rights granted in the Sixth Amendment?
   a. The right to an impartial jury
   b. The right to legal counsel
   c. The right to not self-incriminate
   d. The right to a speedy trial

7. Which of the following was NOT a movement that was going on in the 1960s?
   a. Civil Rights Movement
   b. End the War Movement
   c. Women's Rights Movement
   d. LGBTQ Rights Movement

8. The case of Brown v. Board of Education reversed what landmark Supreme Court doctrine?
    a. Judicial review doctrine
    b. Public safety exception
    c. Due process doctrine
    d. Separate but equal doctrine

Read the following scenario and answer the accompanying question.

The state of South Carolina has new U.S. Census data and is going to draw new lines for congressional voting seats. They come up with a map that has nine districts, with only one being a majority-black district, even though the state is twenty-eight percent black. The Justice Department rejects the map, forcing the South Carolina to draw another map. South Carolina refuses and sues to prevent drawing another map. The court finds in favor of South Carolina, ruling the redrawing of a less reasonable map unconstitutional.

9. The ruling of the court draws upon which Supreme Court case of the same nature?
    a. Shaw v. Reno
    b. Brown v. Board of Education
    c. Tinker v. Des Moines
    d. Plessy v. Ferguson

10. Title IX would aid in which of the following situations?
    a. An African-American woman wanting to vote in her county elections
    b. A factory worker wanting a minimum wage for the work he's doing for the company
    c. A high school girl wanting there to be a girls' soccer team during the fall since there is a boys' team
    d. A first-generation Hispanic teen wanting to go to college but he can't afford it because he doesn't have a college fund

Answer Explanations

1. C: The Bill of Rights grants protections for almost all conceivable parts of life. The Framers were quite adamant that freedom was the ultimate right that the federal government could give to its people, and so they worked hard to ensure that that was exactly what the federal government gave them. Due process is one of those key pieces, guaranteeing every American gets equal protections under the law. Freedom of speech grants this protection too, as one of the more well-known guarantees of the Constitution. The right to a fair and speedy trial is also one of those crucial protections. Right to privacy, however, is not considered one of these protections. While some have recently argued that it is implied, this protection is not explicitly given in the Bill of Rights.

2. A: The term "establishment clause" refers to the part of the First Amendment that applies to freedom of religion. It says: "Congress shall make no law respecting an establishment of religion."

3. B: Our first choice is the subject of another famous case. This one, students wearing bands to protest a war, saw the students winning their case against their school district, so this speech is definitely not restricted. Choice C is also incorrect, as you can protest whatever you want as long as it is peaceful and approved. Choice D is another action that's acceptable, as fliers are okay as long as you are not impeding a war effort. Choice B, however, is libel, and is outlawed as the type of speech that can be restricted and is even punishable by law.

4. A: The NSA's surveillance operation that began under the Patriot Act actually was found to violate only one part of the Bill of Rights. Due process wasn't that distinction, and neither was self-incrimination. Cruel and unusual punishment doesn't fit either. It was found to violate the unlawful search and seizure clause, as the government can't just look at your data without your knowledge.

5. D: As the Supreme Court sought to begin to restrict states from directly contradicting the protections within the Bill of Rights, they were looking at a solution. The Fourteenth Amendment was passed as the answer to those problems, but the Supreme Court had an issue. They had yet to apply it to the states. Total incorporation was lobbied by some justices in the minority but was not the official method they used. Neither was due process; it was one of the protections that the Fourteenth Amendment applied to states. The answer is incrementalism, as the Supreme Court went with this method to apply the amendments one by one to the states.

6. C: The Sixth Amendment is a sweeping amendment that covers a lot of ground in terms of protections for those facing trial. The right to an impartial jury was key to be sure that no bias was in the process. Legal counsel also made sure there was representation for all. The right to a speedy trial was also in the protections. The right to not self-incriminate, however, was not, as that was covered in the previous amendment: the Fifth Amendment.

7. B: The 1960s were a time of growth for the United States. Everyone was pushing for rights and for changes to the system, and people were beginning to challenge the government. The Civil Rights Movement, led by leaders like Martin Luther King Jr., dominated the 1960s leading up to the Civil Rights Act. Women's rights were also key throughout the decade, as well as the movement for LGBTQ rights. End the War was still a decade off, however, with Vietnam still around the corner.

8. D: Brown v. Board of Education set the stage for the fight for civil rights throughout the United States and was the first true rebuff to segregation. Judicial review was one hundred years earlier. The public safety exception has to do with Miranda Rights. The due process doctrine doesn't apply here, either.

That leaves separate but equal, the Plessy v. Ferguson case that the Court overruled, setting the stage for change.

9. A: Brown v. Board of Education (Choice *B*) is a very important case. However, the case deals with the topic of segregation and the reversal of the "separate but equal" doctrine. Tinker v. Des Moines (Choice *C*) gave students the right to protest in schools. While this was an important case, it is not applicable here. Plessy v. Ferguson (Choice *D*) established the idea of "separate but equal." Shaw v. Reno (Choice *A*) made it unconstitutional to use unreasonable maps to connect areas of the same race.

10. C: Title IX was a sweeping law in the 1970s that pushed to extend equal protection for women in the classroom. The law dictated schools with federal funding to provide equal opportunities for women. The correct choice here is *C*, as Title IX pushed schools to increase the number of female sports team.

Unit 4: American Political Ideologies and Beliefs

Methods of Political Analysis

American Core Values

Throughout the life of the United States, there have been debates among the people about what our principles and core values should be. Even at the Constitutional Convention, there wasn't a consensus about the Constitution. But as society grows and changes, certain core values become topics of debate, and also shape how we define ourselves as Americans.

The idea of **individualism** is a bedrock of American ideology, yet what it means to people is different from person to person. Some people believe that government should have no interference in our daily lives, such that the economic and personal sides of our lives should be ours alone. Others believe that the government should only stay away from what's protected in the Constitution, and that anything else is fair game.

Equal opportunity is another key point of our society that sees splits in practice. Some see this as being satisfied as long as freedom is maintained, with the rest being left up to the individual, whereas others, see things like income and family as being hurdles that the government must help to offset to truly give an equal shot.

The idea of the **free market** is also central to our identity in this capitalist economy, but people often disagree with what that actually means. Some people see the need for government protection in the market for it to be free, with blocks and checks for businesses that abuse or get too big. Others see a truly free market as being devoid of government intervention entirely.

Rule of law is a debated topic as well, with splits on the ultimate authority: whether government is the be-all, end-all of enforcement or whether there is a higher citizen calling. **Limited government** sees the same type of debate with a split between those who see the need for governmental intervention in places like healthcare and school and those who think that the best government is one that governs least.

These types of splits in society bleed down into our culture and help create the modern **political culture** of America. These fundamental disagreements can create groups and ideals in parts of our society and drive the national conversation.

Political Socialization

In our society, ideas and debates are everywhere. There are inevitably differences in when and where people grow up in that society and the way in which they do. Such differences craft people into different citizens and construct differing worldviews and perspectives. These splits are very important in determining **political identification**, or what party or interests someone is more likely to identify with.

While not the deciding factors, **demographic characteristics** can be very large indicators of what your belief system may be. These can be anything from your age, race, gender religion, occupation, education level, and anything in between. An example of this can be that, in the current climate in the United States, statistically speaking, people are more likely to be Republicans if they are Christian and more likely to be Democratic if they are a minority voter. These characteristics, while not the only factors, are major factors in your political affiliation and the way in which someone will vote.

Beyond these factors is the idea of **political socialization**. This is the concept of a person developing their political values and ideology through their family, friends, school, church, city, or the media. Political socialization is hugely important in shaping political views and beliefs. Your family can shape the way you feel about many things. Statistically, if your father and mother are Republicans, you also will likely lean in that direction. If you grow up in a Democratic city, you are more likely to be a Democrat.

Your friends are also a heavy influence on how you lean, as you are more likely to model yourself around those you admire, as well as develop relationships with those who have similar ideals. The media also plays a big role. Not only through news and outlets that you might suspect, but also through music and television, as your role models can influence the way you think and perceive the world.

All of these pieces of your life can influence your ideals and political identification and can at least offer an explanation for political scientists to determine the way you might lean.

The Impact of Globalization on the Political Culture in the United States

As the world has grown more interconnected and diverse, the United States has not been immune to the changes. During the twentieth century and continuing into today, the world has changed through the influence of technology and ever-changing policies, as democracy has opened up countries to trade and communication. **Globalization**, or the growth of a new, interconnected world economy culture has changed societies throughout the new world.

More streamlined immigration has exposed the citizens in the United States to diverse cultures and differing peoples. These new people and perspectives have created new segments of political culture on both sides of the spectrum. Exposure to these new people and ideas has created more worldly views than those limited just to thinking of the United States.

Beyond that, expansion of trade between countries has brought an influx of goods and services to the United States that have exposed people to life in other countries. These different services and products have opened people up to the global market and created an avenue for the way of life in other nations to influence thinking and policy making here in the United States.

However, the greatest change to political culture as the result of globalization has been through new media technologies. These are the types of media you are likely exposed to daily: YouTube, social media, books, movies, music, and sports. Such media channels have exposed Americans to the rest of the world and the people in other countries. This newfound perspective of the world has developed new ways to influence American ideals and political culture, with new world players taking interest and influence in our political society. This new and connected world has broadcast the United States' political culture everywhere, while also bringing everyone else to us through different perspectives and ideas.

Generational and Lifecycle Effects Contribute Political Socialization

Beyond the obvious impacts of political socialization, there are others than can shape political ideology and the beliefs of people. One is **generational effects**. Frequently in the news, we hear about the way generations are separated and defined in the media and research. Terms like baby boomers, millennials and Generation Y are easy ways to characterize the different segments of the population born during certain time periods.

However, these separators can be more than just a nickname: in many cases, when we are born can play a large factor in the mindset and ideals that go into the makeup of our political identity. For example, those born around the Vietnam War and coming of age during the protests of the 1960s and 1970s tend to shift toward a more liberal state of political ideology. These people are also more apt to not trust the federal government. Contrast this with people growing up during the Great Depression who were quick to see the federal government as a savior following FDR's presidency and the New Deal. Those who went through World War II are more often more patriotic and embrace the military.

In a similar vein, there are also **lifecycle effects** that can play a heavy impact on political ideology. These are more to do with how where a person is in their life can impact their views on the world and political leanings. For example, a person in their teen years is more apt to be concerned with college costs, wildlife preservation, and perhaps war efforts. Whereas later in life, people are generally more concerned with things like healthcare and insurance. These types of shifts in concerns can guide people into differing political ideologies as they move through life.

The Importance of Major Political Events in Developing Individual Political Attitudes

While both generational and lifecycle effects are large players in political socialization, they are not the only deciding factors. There are other things to keep in mind when considering the development of political attitudes and leanings. One such major contributing factor is **period effects**. These types of effects are centered around major events that happen during the course of someone's life that could impact their feelings about particular political parties and movements. These events can change entire political parties and can shift the conversation nationally to entirely unexpected subjects.

An example of this type of effect in action is the aftermath of the Watergate scandal. During Nixon's presidency, the country became embedded in controversy as the Democratic headquarters in the Watergate hotel was broken into in the months leading into the 1972 reelection campaign of President Nixon. What would transpire over the course of the next couple of years would move the country into conflict and partisanship as more came out about the secret operations of the executive branch in the federal government. The following generations saw a growing distrust of the executive branch as a whole that has extended into today, with more willingness to challenge the president on a variety of issues, regardless of party.

Another example of this type of period effect is the terrorist attacks on September 11, 2001. Following those attacks, approval numbers for President George W. Bush skyrocketed to nearly eighty percent, a stark contrast to Bush's previous forty percent. Americans rallied around the president and saw growing changes to issues that they were concerned about before. Where the debates had been about global warming and domestic issues, concerns quickly turned to overseas worries, with Americans growing increasingly uneasy about national security.

A final example is the Cold War. The idea of impending nuclear war with Russia created fear in Americans. Fear of Russia dominated the minds of Americans and influenced the national debate throughout the 1950s, 1960s, and 1970s. People were concerned about the spread of communism and it became a growing pillar of each political movement to spear the threat. Worries at that time were vastly different than what we've see even just a few decades later, but Americans that grew up in this time carried a fear and sense of patriotism that stemmed from growing up during that period.

Polling Methods to Obtain Public Opinion Data

As the United States has grown and aged, politicians and leaders throughout the nation are constantly worrying about what the electorate and the general population are feeling. As we've grown more connected, it has become easier to gauge this type of interest and shifting opinions on issues. As discussed previously, many factors can influence public opinion and how people vote. Add any number of random events that can impact public opinion and can completely change the national conversation and you've got a political firestorm and system that is constantly in need of self-evaluation by those in charge.

<u>Type of Poll</u>

To gauge public opinion, or just the minds of their constituents, politicians use a variety of polling methods to get a decent guess of where things stand at any given time. Polls come in all shapes and sizes and almost all kinds are widely used and practiced in this political climate.

Opinion polls are some of the more well-known types of polls. This type of polling involves taking a random section of the population. This could be nationwide, statewide, or all the way down to a particular city. People are polled on a particular issue. This is one of the oldest forms of polling and gives politicians an idea of where a particular subset of the population is moving on a particular issue.

Another widely used type of polling is the **benchmark poll**. This type of polling is popular among candidates right before they enter a race or run for a particular office. It gives candidates an early look at how they fare against other candidates or people who might enter a given race. This is typically the first type of poll run before someone enters a political campaign or before reelection efforts.

Tracking polls are similar to benchmark polls, but they are polls run over a distinct period of time that give people an idea of how a candidate or idea has fared over a set period of time. For example, a candidate may change their messaging to try and appeal to a wider set of voters and may use tracking polls to see the effect it is having over a set timeframe, as a way of deciding whether to keep the strategy or not.

Entrance polling and **exiting polling** also give a good idea of standing on voting day. As the names suggest, entrance polling is polling conducted before people go in to vote on Election Day, while exit polling is done when voters leave the booth. These techniques are very popular on the day of elections for obvious reasons and give candidates a good idea of the results before polls close.

<u>Sampling Techniques</u>

Samples are the most important piece of any polling. Samples are the parts of the population you are surveying. There are two main sampling techniques used in polling. The first is **random sampling**. This takes the population and gives everyone an equal chance of being selected. It renders a truly random result but may not always be the best representation of the general populace. The second is **stratified sampling**. This is a more encompassing sampling design that groups the population in subsets and weighs demographics and different populations.

Identifying who you want to poll is very important. You could want a national gauge of voters, or to see how you're doing with African-American voters, or possibly see how a candidate is doing with certain groups of voters in a particular part of state. Once you've decided who you are looking to poll, the type of survey used can play a big factor in your data set. One way is through a **mass survey**. This is as it sounds: polling many different voters on a particular issue or candidate to see what the results are. This contrasts with **focus groups**, which are designed to take pieces of the population and get them into a room to elicit their feelings on particular issues or ideas.

<u>Type and Format of Questions</u>
After you've decided on your audience and participants, the types of questions and format of polling is very important. Questions can frame answers in very different ways. For example, framing your question as asking if you support a particular military action will get a very different response than framing the question as, "Do you support the needless war in Vietnam?" Answers will vary. Format also plays a factor, as stacking repeating questions can skew results and give different answers.

One last thing to keep in mind for polling is the idea of **sampling error**. This can happen in a variety of ways. It could be in picking too much of one demographic, from polling too many of one belief, from polling by phone in the middle of the day when people are more likely to be working, and anything in between.

Factors that Affect the Relationship Between Scientific Polling and Elections

Despite all of the ways to conduct and track polls in political races and on certain issues, there still is a massive disconnect between polling and actual practice in the field. Throughout the political arena, we've seen errors in political polling. Famously, the media at large took a brunt of criticism for the polling surrounding the presidential election in 2016. In addition, we consistently see candidates reacting differently to national polling. For example, raises in minimum wage are generally popular nationally, but few run on this message during election efforts. So why is polling sometimes so wacky?

Public opinion is massively important in political life, but it can be misleading. Sometimes, poll results vary across platforms. This can be attributed to a variety of reasons. One is errors in sampling techniques. This might be from sampling too many Republicans or too much of one area of the country, for example. There may also be biased questions, as discussed earlier, or flawed questioning strategies that give slanted answers. There can also be issues in small sample sizes, which can skew results. However, large sample sizes can also have bad influences as they can increase the margin for error in a poll, furthering the questionability of the poll.

Polling can be a strong method for politicians to get a grip on public opinion and try and see where things stand for their campaign or on a particular issue. However, given the biases and questionable trustworthiness of some polls, politicians sometimes forego what's perceived as public opinion and follow their own instincts. While trusted polls have solid methods, there is simply a massive amount of data to try and comb through to get a good measure of where the public actually stands on an issue.

Competing Policy-Making Interests

The Democratic and Republican Parties

There are two major political parties in the United States. These parties dominate the political process and control each part of the government. By and large, most Americans end up voting for one of the two major parties in each election, from the local and state level all the way up to the federal level. While the parties have changed over the years, the two are defined in a fairly solid way today.

The **Democratic Party** (known sometimes by D or DEM) is the oldest party in the United States, founded in 1828 by Andrew Jackson. While changing over the years, today's Democrats tend to follow the **liberal ideology**. Modern-day liberalism broadly believes in government intervention in the economic interests of the country. They also believe that the government functions to ensure the social standing of its people and to enforce equality. They do not believe in government intervention in social parts of life. This ideology is the "left" wing of political spectrum. Many people use the term "**progressive**" to also describe today's liberal.

The **Republican Party** (R or GOP) is the other major political party, founded in 1854. Republicans function with the **conservative ideology**, believing in a small and minimal government. They believe that the government should not be involved in the economy. Beyond this, they tend to believe that the government should restrict things like same-sex marriage and abortion. Republicans are referred to as the "right wing" of the political spectrum.

Beyond these two major groups, there are various other political parties. **Libertarians** are the third-biggest political party, believing in the limited government that Framers envisioned. The **Green Party** is another party, believing in a strong federal government. There are also the **communitarians**, who believe that communities should be thought of over individuals. Additionally, **nationalists** believe in the nation over all others and tend to fall on the far end of either political wing.

Public Policies Reflect the Politically-Active Members of the Diverse Society

While the United States is dominated by a two-party system that seems to fit into a neat little spectrum, the reality is that the country is made up of people that fall all along this imaginary line. The makeup of American elections is even more skewed, with different people making up the actual voting electorate than citizens who are eligible to vote. This glaring gap in the actual populace and likely voters is always amplified during general elections.

To give further clarification, it is widely known that older Americans tend to vote at a higher rate than younger Americans. During the 2016 election, a far larger percentage of eligible voters aged 55–64 voted than those aged 18–24. What this presents is a situation where politicians are much more likely to target older Americans than their younger counterparts, as more of them are likely to actually show up to the polls and vote. Because those under the age of 18 are not eligible to vote, politicians often tend not to put significant weight or energy on targeting the youngest sector of the population.

Particular movements can carry heavy weight because they can mobilize better than others, giving them a bigger seat at the table than they might otherwise have if the entire population was actually voting. Things like these may tip the scales toward a particular movement, candidate, or idea that otherwise might not have been voted in and implemented if the entire population voted, rather than the historical average of around fifty percent.

Put simply by writer Aaron Sorkin: "Decisions are made by those who show up."

Balancing Individual Liberty and Governmental Efforts to Promote Stability

At the heart of the divide between Republicans and Democrats over time has been the role of individual liberty. Both parties teach their defense of this particular right granted in the Constitution, but the way they do so is quite different. They've changed over time with different proposals and initiatives that each has supported.

For example, the Democrats have long been supporters of individual liberty for the person. This includes being against governmental intervention in personal lives. They believe in government staying out of sexual issues, as well as marriage and issues like marijuana regulation. They believe that individual freedom equates to protecting privacy and what people do in their day-to-day lives. However, they believe that the government must provide stability in the market and regulations on businesses.

In contrast, Republicans use individual liberty in the economy. Republicans believe that the government should remove itself from the free market system, allowing businesses and their workers to regulate themselves free of governmental regulation and undue burdens. Further, they believe taxes are a burden on Americans and they must be lifted for people to be truly free. However, in personal lives, Republicans believe that the government must enforce a certain morality. This includes intervening against abortion and same-sex marriage.

These differences have resulted in friction on a variety of issues. The tax cuts passed under George W. Bush were praised by Republicans as improvements in the individual freedom of Americans to spend their own money, while Democrats attacked it for removing the ability of lower income families to get the help that the government can provide them.

Beyond that, Democrats have made pushes toward individual freedom with recent efforts to provide a national healthcare marketplace. They argue that limiting the costs of insurance can give people more freedom to take care of themselves, while Republicans argue that this is government infringement on the free market.

Liberal, Conservative, and Libertarian Ideologies

As discussed, the economic marketplace is a place of much contention between the major political parties. Each of them possesses different ideas on how the market should run. They also disagree on which type of marketplace would best function for everyday Americans.

Liberals believe that greater governmental regulation is the only way to ensure fairness and openness between the businesses. They also support worker protections like minimum wage, unions, and restrictions on firing and hiring by employers. Liberals believe that governmental intervention is necessary to prevent businesses and corporations from taking advantage of consumers and their workers, as has happened at different periods in the history of the United States.

In contrast, **conservatives** believe that a system with fewer regulations would be the best way forward. They believe in limitations on governmental restrictions, including opposing higher minimum wages and more regulations on banks and financial institutions. They believe that regulations hurt businesses and don't help the economy grow, instead favoring just the government and the collection of tax money.

Libertarians are a further distinction from the conservative ideology. Libertarians don't believe in any regulations or governmental intervention on the economic side of issues. Libertarians believe only in the governmental need for protection of property rights and voluntary trade. Beyond these protections, libertarians believe that the marketplace should be left alone, just as it was at the founding of the country and how the Framers would have intended the economy to be managed.

Ideological Differences on Marketplace Regulation

The debate about governmental intervention in the marketplace is a relatively new phenomenon. Throughout the first century of the United States, the government left the economy mostly alone, aside from spending that the government needed. That changed in the early part of the twentieth century, however, when people began to lean on the government for protections during the Second Industrial

Revolution as companies provided less than ideal work conditions for their workers. This amplified during the Great Depression, as the government had to pull the economy out of a major collapse.

Since that intervention, the government has taken an active role in economic policy. This new intervention is based on the liberal ideal of **Keynesian economics**, which underlines the need for governmental spending and intervention to promote economic growth. This type of thinking caused the birth of a regulatory body called the **Federal Reserve** that has served as the government's agency that guides monetary and fiscal policy. The "Fed" as it's known today, regulates banks and pushes for economic growth.

Monetary policy is the government's methods of controlling the national money supply to influence the economy. This also involves the government using interest rates on borrowing money to try and influence the growth and buying of Americans in the economy. **Fiscal policy** differs slightly in that it is the government's ability to influence the economy through taxation and spending, normally through buying particular goods for trade or lifting taxation on certain items to influence buying patterns. Both Congress and the president try to use these ways to influence the economy through both growth and recessions with spending bills and executive orders designed to push things along.

This is not to say that the system isn't without protesters. Modern conservative members attack this way of governing by arguing for **supply-side economics**. This type of economic philosophy states the idea that the economy may only grow and succeed if the government lifts regulations and decreases taxes. Republicans have adopted this type of philosophy since the 1970s as a way to try to limit governmental interference in business and the economy, typically arguing that it is the only way for the market to grow.

Ideological Differences on Personal Privacy

Social policy is another hot button issue between the major parties in the United States. Social policy embraces policies that relate to education, healthcare, criminal justice, inequality, and human services. These issues are debated ad nauseum between the parties and are nuanced by their support on either side.

Liberals tend to advocate for the **right to privacy**, or the restriction of governmental interference into someone's private beliefs and the way they live their life. They believe that the government should stay away from regulation of marriage and sexual relations, as well as move away from criminalizing things like marijuana. However, liberals do support governmental intervention to prevent inequality. Liberals believe that the government must serve as a protector against discrimination and that it must protect workers. They also believe in a smaller military and fewer restrictions on immigration.

Conservatives, however, generally oppose governmental intervention in the relationship between businesses and employees. They also don't believe governmental intervention is needed to address economic inequality broadly, believing that less could be more for many Americans. Conservatives also believe in the protections of individual liberties—those that are protected in the Bill of Rights—mainly the Second Amendment's right to bear arms. They do, however, support governmental intervention in certain social issues. They believe in the criminalization of marijuana, as well as restrictions on same-sex marriage. They also believe in a strong military and strict restriction on immigration.

Libertarians again fall on the farther end of the conservative wing. They believe that there should be no governmental intervention in social policy at all, only property rights and free trade need protections.

Governmental Involvement Policy Trends Reflect the Success of Political Parties

Both sides of the spectrum have seen victories in their version of where they think the government should place itself in social policy.

Liberals have seen victories in minimum wage requirements, and healthcare protections in the expansion of Medicare and Medicaid, as well as in food stamps and unemployment benefits. Their policies have seen limited decriminalization of marijuana and criminal justice reforms at different points in American history.

Conservatives have seen victories as well. They have ushered in deregulations of banks and Wall Street, tax cuts in almost every decade, consistent growth of the military, and strict limits on drugs.

Both parties have seen ebbs and flows throughout different transitions of power that continue to shift back and forth from the beginning through to today.

Practice Questions

1. Which of the following is NOT a demographic characteristic that could be an indicator of your political ideology?
   a. Your age
   b. Your religion
   c. Your favorite sport
   d. Your occupation

2. A candidate is thinking of speaking out on an issue but is worried because of the political makeup of her district. What type of poll or survey would NOT be useful for her to conduct before speaking out on this issue?
   a. Benchmark poll
   b. Opinion poll
   c. Mass survey
   d. Tracking poll

3. The day of the election in his district, an incumbent congressman is beginning to worry about his chances. He has run a campaign on a controversial issue and worries that he may not have fared as well as his internal polling may have him believe, and he's worried of his constituents' opinion on his new platform. To ease his mind, he sends a staffer to the voting precinct to poll voters before they go in about whom they are voting for. What type of polling did the congressman conduct?
   a. Mass survey
   b. Benchmark poll
   c. Opinion poll
   d. Entrance poll

4. A ballot initiative is up for vote today in California. The interest group organizing the initiative is excited but wants to be reassured of their confidence in the initiative. They reach out to a polling firm to gauge how their prospects were looking. The firm concluded that the initiative was fifty-eight percent likely to pass. However, on the day of the election, it failed with only forty-one percent of the vote. Which of the following is NOT one of the ways the sample may have erred?
   a. The poll sample was too large
   b. The poll sample was stratified
   c. The poll sample was too small
   d. The poll had poor questioning methods

5. Which of the following is a generational effect that can define your political identification?
   a. Your mother talks to you about her views on same-sex marriage
   b. Growing up during the Cold War
   c. You become concerned about college tuition costs as you begin senior year of high school
   d. Being in New York for the 9/11 terrorist attacks

6. Which of the following is NOT one of the major political parties?
   a. Nationalist
   b. Republican
   c. Libertarian
   d. Democratic

7. Which of the following is NOT a liberal policy?
    a. Legalization of marijuana
    b. Lowering of taxes
    c. More regulation on Wall Street
    d. Raising of the minimum wage

8. Which party or ideology would MOST agree with the statement: "The government that governs best is a government that governs least"?
    a. Conservatives
    b. Democrats
    c. Progressives
    d. Green Party

9. What is the name for the movement, started in the 1970s, that began the conservative pushback against the increasing role the government was taking in the economy?
    a. Fiscal policy
    b. Keynesian economics
    c. Fiscal responsibility
    d. Supply-side economics

10. You are the owner of a medium-sized accounting firm in New York City. You have grown increasingly tired of governmental interference in your business and have decided to use your vote to make a change. You are tired of regulations and taxes and are looking to end the burden of them completely. Which candidate are you voting for?
    a. Progressive
    b. Democratic
    c. Republican
    d. Libertarian

Answer Explanations

1. C: There are many ways to shape your political ideology. In fact, as we grow, almost everything can shape those opinions that develop in our minds all the way until today. Your demographic characteristics, however, are a little more personal. Your age is certainly one, with that often playing a factor in your beliefs and concerns. Your religion is big as well, and a demographic factor. Your occupation is also part of your demographic makeup, while the sport you like, which is part of your personality, is not a demographic characteristic.

2. A: If a candidate wanted to poll for an issue before dipping her toe in the water (a common occurrence), there are a few different options available. The opinion poll is useful, as it literally gives polling data on the opinion right then and there. While mass surveys are a little less reliable, they would certainly give a good idea of her district's preference. Tracking polls would probably give the best idea, as they would show the progression over time. A benchmark poll would be of no help, however, as it would just give opinions on the candidate.

3. D: The entrance poll is correct, as he's gathering information before voters go into the booth. The congressman's staffer isn't conducting a mass survey, although he's probably talking to a good number of people. A benchmark poll is with potential voters; whereas an entrance poll is with definite voters since they are headed into the polling location. An opinion poll isn't correct either, as the staffer isn't asking about a particular issue.

4. B: Samples can be off in a variety of ways. A poll that is too large can skew data and can make the margin for error larger. Polls that are too small are often not representative of the electorate at large. Poor questioning methods can skew the answers in a way that may not give the right view on the particular issue. Stratified polling, however, is one of the safest and most practiced polling methods around.

5. B: In the life of a typical American, there can be many potential effects on your political ideology. Generational effects, however, generally involve what's going on in a key part of your life. Your mother's views aren't generational effects. Your concerns about tuition are a lifecycle effect. The New York terror attacks is a period effect. Growing up in the Cold War, however, is a generational effect.

6. A: Nationalists may exist on both ends of the political spectrum. However, they aren't a political party, just an ideology.

7. B: Liberals generally tend to only want governmental interference when it comes to inequality and the marketplace. They want strong federal power, but only to protect certain safeguards they deem necessary. Legalization of marijuana certainly falls into their belief in rights of privacy. Regulation of Wall Street is also in their wheelhouse. The raising of minimum wage is something they've pushed for a long time. Lowering of taxes, however, is generally not pushed for by liberal voters.

8. A: To answer this question, you must separate those that believe in a limited government. Democrats don't fit that mold. Neither do progressives, as that is another term for liberals, the main ideology of the Democratic Party. The Green Party also believes in a strong federal government. Conservatives believe in limited government, so this quote would definitely fall in line with their ideology.

9. D: Fiscal policy is the term for what the government decides to do when it comes to its impact on the economy. Keynesian economics is the liberal economic belief that says that the government should have a role in the economy. Fiscal responsibility refers to taxation and government spending. Supply-side economics is the correct answer, as it refers to the pushback against government in the economy.

10. D: If you're the owner, you want the candidate who is going to get the government most fully out of your business. That means the progressive and the Democratic candidate are out. While the Republican candidate would believe in limiting regulation, they aren't fully for getting government out of things completely. The Libertarian candidate, however, wants the government completely out and would be your choice.

Unit 5: Political Participation

Methods of Political Analysis

Expansion of Political Opportunities

Constitutional amendments and federal legislation have exponentially expanded political participation in the United States. At its founding, the United States limited political participation to white men and some states further restricted participation to white male property owners. Following the Civil War, Congress passed the **Fifteenth Amendment** (1870) to prohibit denying the vote based on "race, color, or previous condition of servitude." This amendment was passed along with the **Thirteenth** and **Fourteenth Amendments**, collectively called the **Reconstruction Amendments**, but the effort to expand political participation for African Americans largely failed in large stretches of the country for nearly another century. In response to the Reconstruction Amendments, most Southern states passed **Jim Crow laws** to prevent African Americans from participating in the political process, and the federal government failed to act. Congress ultimately enacted federal legislation like the **Civil Rights Act of 1964** and **Voting Rights Act of 1965** to enforce the Fourteenth and Fifteenth Amendments. In addition, the states ratified the **Twenty-Fourth Amendment** (1964) to prohibit poll taxes, which Southern states had used for a century to deny legal voting rights to African American, lower-income citizens, and other people those states deemed undesirable.

During the early twentieth century, the **Seventeenth Amendment** (1913) expanded political participation by establishing the popular election of U.S. Senators. Prior to the Seventeenth Amendment, state legislatures had handpicked U.S. Senators, which allowed for far less input from the public. Less than a decade later during the aftermath of World War I, the **Nineteenth Amendment** (1920) prohibited denying the right to vote on the basis of sex.

The **Twenty-Sixth Amendment** (1971) also expanded public participation by prohibiting the denial of voting rights based on age. This amendment was passed after Vietnam War protestors applied immense public pressure to lower the legal voting age. Prior to the Twenty-Sixth Amendment, the voting age was twenty-one but anyone eighteen or older was eligible for the military draft.

Models of Voting Behavior

Political scientists have tried to promulgate a series of theories to analyze why citizens vote the way they do. These theories include: rational-choice voting, retrospective voting, prospective voting, and party-line voting. Each theory shares in common the attempt to understand past and future voting behavior. An individual voter might be motivated by one theory above all or they might have more mixed motivations for voting. Many voters are motivated by several theories at the same time, while some voters naturally follow a single approach to voting.

Rational-choice voting explains voting behavior based on individual interests. For example, if a voter's number one priority is lowering taxes, then a rational-choice voter would vote for the candidate offering the lowest taxes rates. **Retrospective voting** means the voter is deciding based on past performance. So, if that same voter didn't think their incumbent representative had kept their promise to decrease taxes, then they might seek out an alternative or abstain from the political process altogether. **Prospective voting** is voting based on future performance. These candidates judge politicians based on the likelihood of their representative executing their campaign promises. All voters expect their representatives to follow through on their promises but prospective voters behave more pragmatically than the average voter. For example, if the politician who is most aligned with their personal interest is unlikely to win or execute that vision, then a prospective voter might more strongly consider their second most aligned candidate. **Party-line voting** is unique in that it places all of the emphasis on the political party, not individual candidates or specific issues, so these voters only ever vote for one political party. Party-line voters are the most likely group to vote against their own interests as it's unlikely that they will be aligned with their political party on every single issue.

Structural Barriers to Turnout

Along with demographics and effectiveness of representation, voter turnout is relatively low in the United States. It is rather rare for voter turnout to exceed sixty percent for an American election, and no election has surpassed sixty-five percent turnout since 1916. This diminished voter turnout is due to structural barriers, voter registration laws, voting procedures, and types of elections.

Structural barriers relate to how socioeconomic conditions disproportionately restrict the voter turnout based on a shared characteristic, like class status or race. For example, voters in lower-income districts often receive insufficient resources for an election. In practice, this results in longer lines that pose an even greater strain on workers. Low-income voters have less flexibility to miss work because missing hours poses a threat to daily needs. So, if standing an extra hour in line means missing one hour of work, resulting in literally less food on the table, the incentive structure is geared toward work, not voting. The United States has historically and repeatedly erected legal barriers to prevent voting based on race. While the Civil Rights Movement succeeded in tearing down considerable barriers, communities of color continue to receive relatively fewer resources to hold elections, resulting in smaller turnout.

Voter registration laws and other electoral procedures deter voters and entrench structural barriers. States and local governments hold the constitutional power to hold and oversee the electoral process, so there's tremendous variance in voter registration and electoral procedures. For example, some states may automatically register citizens based on taxes or participation in a government program or service, while others might require a citizen to send a form or physically go to an office. Although seemingly slight, the extra time to register to vote serves as a deterrent to people who are less able to miss time from work. Many **voting procedures** function the same way, such as the various voter identification laws seen across the country. The requirements range from government photo identification to any form of photographic identification along with a bill or paystub. Elderly voters, low-income voters, and people of color are less likely to have photo identification than other socioeconomic groups, so the harm is disproportionate.

Voter turnout is also always much higher for presidential elections when compared to mid-terms. Lacking the attraction of a presidential race, less than half of the electorate typically votes in the mid-term elections. For example, the presidential election of 2012 had a 58.2 percent voter turnout, but the 2014 mid-term elections had 36.7 percent voter turnout. The absence of presidential candidates makes voters feel as if the mid-term elections are less important even though Congress and local government have just as much or more impact on people's lives as the president. In addition, low voter turnout during the mid-term elections can undermine a sitting president, particularly if the president's party loses control over the Senate or House of Representatives during the mid-terms.

Demographics Can Impact Turnout and Engagement

Demographics and political efficacy are strong indicators of how likely an individual is to vote. Generally speaking, non-Hispanic white citizens are more likely to vote than any other racial group; non-Hispanic black citizens have the second highest turnout; and Hispanic citizens have the third highest turnout. Much of this trend can be explained based on the historic barriers placed on nonwhite voters and the present-day wealth gap between nonwhite and white households. There are also some election policies that increase white turnout over other groups. For example, some states have stringent voter ID laws, and white voters are significantly more likely to have the proper ID than nonwhite voters.

In regard to age, the older the voter, then the more likely they will vote. For example, in the 2016 presidential election turnout among voters older than sixty years of age exceeded seventy percent, which was higher than any other age group. In contrast, turnout among voters between the ages of eighteen and twenty-nine was approximately forty-five percent in that same election. Political scientists also consider the effect of education, income, gender, and marital status. While this demographic analysis is useful for predicting the turnout for large groups, it's important to remember that it isn't an exact science. Past turnout doesn't guarantee future turnout, especially during unprecedented campaigns. For example, the first African American president in American history, Barack Obama, achieved nearly unprecedented turnout among African Americans and young voters.

Voter turnout is also relatively low in the United States due to **political efficacy**, which is defined as voter's faith and trust in elected officials to deliver desired outcomes. As a result, low political efficacy drives voter apathy. Twenty-first century electoral politics have been divisive, and perhaps more importantly, both major political parties have been largely ineffective at achieving campaign commitments after taking office. Consequently, anger at both major political parties is increasingly common, and the present electoral system undermines the development of third parties. With limited appealing options, many Americans drop out of the political process, particularly during mid-term elections.

Factors that Influence Voter Choice

Citizens decide how to vote based on a variety of issues, including party identification, ideological orientation, candidate characteristics, contemporary political issues, and demographics.

Party Identification
Voters who identify with a political party are significantly more likely to vote for that party's candidate. Although straight-ticket voting has declined since the 1960s, party identification continues to be one of the most important factors in how voters approach elections. Similarly, ideological orientation influences how voters perceive political issues and candidates. For example, a citizen holding to a socialist ideology will favor socially and fiscally progressive candidates, be wary of liberal Democratic establishment candidates, and almost never vote for conservative Republican candidates. Ideological orientation often works in tandem with party identification because voters choose their political party affiliation based on the party's ideology.

Candidate Characteristics
Individual candidates' charisma, policies, and vision can increase voter turnout based on a desire to vote for that candidate. In addition, individual politicians can sometimes attract people from other political bases or demographics that don't typically vote for that candidate's political party or ideology. For example, a significant number of Americans voted for Democrat Barack Obama in 2008 and 2012 and conservative Republican Donald Trump in 2016. These candidates could not be more opposite based on party identification, political ideology, and stances on issues; however, they were still individually attractive to the same voters.

Contemporary Political Issues

Contemporary political issues also influence how citizens vote. Most candidates share the same stances on political issues as their party establishment, so differences on contemporary political issues are more important for how citizens vote during primaries held between candidates from the same political party. In addition, some voters are single issue voters. For example, a voter who prioritizes abortion above all else will almost never vote for a politician with conflicting views regardless of political identification or ideology.

Demographic Characteristics

Demographics are a valuable predictor of how citizens vote. Demographic considerations include: ethnicity, education, gender, income, race, religion, and sex. Some demographic trends have remained constant for decades, while others have changed dramatically due to historical trends. For example, low-income white voters had been a core part of the Democratic base until the twenty-first century when this demographic trend reversed. Now, low-income white voters are increasingly entrenched in the Republican Party. Some demographic trends are fluid based on the specific election, such as educational achievement. Both the Republican and Democratic parties compete for voters who have achieved higher levels of education, so educational achievement is usually a weaker predictor of voter choice than other demographic trends, such as race and religion.

Competing Policy-Making Interests

Linkage Institutions Allow Communication with Various Channels

Citizens must be able to communicate with representatives and be able to participate politically in order for representative government to function. The channels of communication between representatives, political staff, and constituents are called **linkage institutions**.

Political parties exist to win elections and maximize power in government in order to enact their policy platform. Citizens support the party by voting for the party's candidates or by working directly within the party structure. Most political parties, including both major political parties like the Republicans and Democrats and smaller political parties like the Libertarian Party and Democratic Socialists of America, have a leadership and organizational structure. The larger political parties have local officers where party members can directly engage with the party as an activist, volunteer organizer, or staff member.

In theory, the largest political parties with the strongest linkage institutions should be the most successful political institutions. However, this isn't always the case because political parties can be undermined by conflicts of interest with interest groups and/or the disruption of communication channels. Some interest groups openly collaborate with political parties, including the governing political party, but they also disrupt the party's function as a linkage institution with grassroots support ("the base").

Elections are the best opportunity for individuals to communicate their political preferences. Losing political parties and interest groups will often spend considerable time and money on why they lost and how they could better appeal to voters. Media represents another linkage institution, connecting citizens with political parties and government. Specifically, the media allows citizens to directly engage with candidates and representatives, especially since the rise of social media. Political parties, interest groups, and governments have also capitalized on the modern media environment's reach by driving discussions on social media and sending surrogates to defend policies on traditional media, like television and print.

Function and Impact of Political Parties

Political parties play a pivotal role and exert considerable influence over the electorate and government. Active politicians and elite party leadership ("the establishment") oversee the planning and execution of the party's broad electoral and governing strategy in the media, voter outreach, and actual policymaking. While political parties overwhelmingly favor their own candidates over rival political parties' candidates, conflicts within a political party do occur. These internal conflicts can directly influence political parties' role and influence on the electorate and government.

The mobilization and education of voters is how political parties win elections and consolidate political power. Rather than waiting for the electorate to make a decision in a vacuum, political parties rally the troops around important issues, particularly those issues with the most support among the party's base. Mobilization includes everything from registering voters for upcoming elections to getting issues trending on social media. In effect, mobilization is priming the electorate to take action whether it's to vote or protest a piece of legislation.

Party platforms are an effective tool for mobilizing and educating voters because they are a summary of what the political party hopes to achieve. So, the potential voters who most agree with the platform are the optimal targets for mobilization efforts because they are the most likely to vote. Feedback from the electorate can also cause parties to tweak their platform, which can change how politicians govern once in power. The potential for reelection incentivizes politicians to enact as much of their party's platform as possible because voters theoretically use the platform as a benchmark for success. If a politician only enacts a small portion of a popular platform, they are unlikely to win reelection unless they can shift the blame to some other individual or entity.

Political parties exercise control over who wins elections through the selection process and management of campaigns. Parties select the candidates who are the most likely to win elections. However, the establishment might differ with the base on who they consider to be "electable" and/or how much electability should be weighed when deciding between competing candidates. For example, the base might prefer an ideologue while the establishment desires someone closer to the center to attract swing voters. Political parties justifiably pursue candidates with strong fundraising skills because they fear candidates with limited resources will be unable to break through to the electorate. At the same time, overemphasizing fundraising can turn off voters and even harm the function of government if the candidates violate campaign finance laws. Political parties also assist candidates with their media strategy during elections, including the funding, planning, and executing of messages. This function can lead to further conflict between candidates and the party establishment when there's disagreement over messaging.

Candidate-Centered Campaigns

American political parties' role has changed over the years. Prior to the Progressive Era in the late nineteenth and early twentieth century, state legislatures nominated their party's presidential candidates and party officials were extremely influential in selecting down ballot candidates. The expression "smoke-filled rooms" is often used as shorthand for this type of selection process where political party elites would make all of the decisions behind closed doors. In the present-day, political parties continue to have an important role and significant influence on their candidates. For example, the Democratic Party practice of sending unpledged delegates (super delegates) to nominating conventions dates back to the "smoke-filled room" era because these super delegates are typically loyal to the party leadership. Super delegates are especially influential because they can decide to support a candidate earlier in the race, making it appear that one candidate is a heavy favorite to win before they are very far in the lead based on primary victories.

As a result of these historical changes and the modern media environment, campaigns have become increasingly candidate driven over the last several decades. Barack Obama's 2008 and 2012 campaigns were particularly notable for their conflict with party leadership over who ultimately controlled the campaign contributions. More than even the money or strategic differences, the struggle was about how much power a party's presidential candidate should exercise over that party's leadership. Donald Trump's 2016 presidential campaign illustrated an even further departure from "smoke-filled rooms." Much of the Republican Party establishment refused to fully embrace Trump as the party's nominee until his victory in the 2016 presidential election. Following that election, parts of that leadership have essentially left the Republican Party, calling themselves "Never Trumpers," but they lacked meaningful support among Republican base. In effect, Donald Trump's candidacy effectively seized the Republican Party establishment, largely because Donald Trump is individually more popular with the Republican base than any other Republican politician or party member.

Policy Modifications to Appeal to Voters

In addition to the trend toward candidate-centered campaigns during recent elections, political parties often try to make their policies and messaging appeal to various demographic coalitions. Changes to messaging aren't always reflected in the actual policies if the policy change would threaten part of the political party's coalition. Likewise, when appealing to different components of a coalition, parties and candidates will emphasize different policies. However, merely changing the messaging risks losing the support of a different part of the coalition.

For example, over the last two decades, the Republican Party's coalition has begun to more heavily feature the white working class. The white working class had previously been part of the Democratic coalition as constructed by President Franklin Delano Roosevelt. Richard Nixon's "Southern Strategy" was the first major Republican concentrated attempt to garner support from the white working class, and those efforts continued through the Reagan administration and into the present day. As a result, the Republican Party has adjusted its messaging from fiscal conservatism to focus more on immigration and political correctness, which are both more attractive to the white working class than slashing social safety nets. As such, President Donald Trump's immigration rhetoric represents the culmination of decades-old demographic trends more than a sudden policy departure. While the rest of the Republican coalition might not agree with this messaging or policy program, the establishment remains committed to other policy pursuits, like tax cuts for businesses. This illustrates how political parties must balance superficial messaging with policy changes when dealing with the complexities of a complex political coalition.

Structural Changes to Political Parties

The structure of political parties has changed as a result of regional realignments, campaign finance law, and technological changes.

Regional realignments are most often caused by critical elections, changes to the party's policies, and demographic shifts within the party's constituency. The Republican Party transitioned from a single-issue party into a major political party during the election of 1860. In the preceding decades, the Whig Party collapsed, and this loss of a major political party left a power vacuum for the Republicans, especially in the North where their anti-slavery platform was most popular. Following Republican Abraham Lincoln's victory in the 1860 election and the Civil War, the Republicans consolidated power in the North and competed with Democrats in the South. President Franklin Delano Roosevelt's victory in the 1932 election resulted in another major regional realignment. President Roosevelt's New Deal coalition united the South's white working class with the North's industrial centers. Additionally, the New Deal coalition attracted African Americans to the Democratic Party for the first time.

Policy shifts can also change voter constituencies, resulting in political realignments. The last regional realignment occurred after the Republican Party implemented its **Southern Strategy**, an intentional shift in policy. The Southern Strategy radically altered the Republicans' constituency and limited its future options. Prior to the 1950s, the Republican Party still enjoyed considerable support within the African American community. Compared to the Republican Party's historic opposition to slavery, the Southern Strategy represented a radical departure because it involved supporting Jim Crow laws and opposing the Civil Rights Movement. The goal was to regain control over the South and Midwest by appealing to the white working class. This policy shift was largely successful as an electoral strategy. Richard Nixon exploited the Southern Strategy to win two presidential elections, including a landslide victory in 1972. However, as the white working class became increasingly entrenched in the Republican Party, the establishment enjoyed less flexibility in adopting pro-immigration policies, like amnesty. When the Republican establishment attempted to reach a bipartisan compromise on immigration in 2013 and 2014, the base revolted and several high-profile congressional leaders lost primaries over immigration. In effect, the decision to pursue a new constituency altered what policies the establishment could pursue without losing their political coalition.

Campaign finance laws changes parties' structure by turning partisan politics into a multi-billion dollar business. The Supreme Court's decision in *Citizens United v. FEC* (2010) ruled that campaign contributions were free speech, effectively allowing individuals and corporate entities to contribute unlimited money to Super PACs. This ruling exacerbated the already climbing costs for election cycles. For example, $6.5 billion was spent on the 2016 presidential and congressional races, and the presidential election alone cost more than $2.4 billion. Consequently, political parties now closely resemble multinational corporations with the ability to generate billions of dollars in "revenue" and employ thousands of employees located in officers all over the country.

Similarly, technological changes have altered the electoral landscape and forced political parties to compete in the digital space for the purpose of seeking a competitive advantage over rival political parties. The twenty-first century's Digital Revolution has resulted in an exponential explosion in data, and voter data management tools can now provide instantaneous access to contact information and voter profiles for all party members. Some tools even incorporate voter profiles for every prospective voter in the electorate. Rather than producing a handful of television commercials, political parties and candidates can tailor advertisements specifically to voters' values and key issues. These tools are at the center of the controversies surrounding the 2016 election. The Russian government stole and exploited finely tailored voter profiles to hack the electorate by exploiting divisions to sow discord and chaos. The Internet further provides political parties and candidates with unprecedented opportunities to communicate with constituents, disseminate information, raise awareness, and mobilize voters. Now, feedback on political platforms, messaging, policies, and legislation can be gathered in real time.

Structural Barriers to Third-Party and Independent Candidates

Unlike proportional electoral systems, which allow voters to rank candidates based on preference, the United States mostly uses a first-past-the-poll electoral system. Under this system, citizens can only express a preference for one candidate per office, and voting districts are winner-take-all. This electoral system poses a structural barrier to third-party and independent candidates.

When there are only two viable candidates, a vote for a third candidate is essentially a wasted vote. As such, citizens are forced into choosing the better of two evils to prevent their least desirable candidate from winning. The success of third parties can spoil a major political party's electoral chances. For example, Theodore Roosevelt's Progressive Party split the Republican vote in the presidential election of 1912, and it resulted in the underdog Democratic candidate, Woodrow Wilson, winning the election. Consequently, major political parties often seek to preempt the rise of third-party challengers by incorporating popular third-party policies.

Occasionally emergent third-parties overtake a struggling major party, like the anti-slavery Republican party succeeding the Whigs, but if the third-party or independent candidate's platform is popular, one of the major political parties will incorporate planks of that platform to undermine the challenger. Co-opting popular policies can also consolidate political power against the other major political party. Most famously, the Progressive Party split with the Republican Party during the 1912 presidential election, and Theodore Roosevelt became the first and only third-party candidate to win more popular votes than both major party candidates. However, the Progressive Party ultimately collapsed as the Democrats and Republicans incorporated much of the Progressive platform, leading to a political reunion between the two major political parties and Progressive voters. For example, President Woodrow Wilson's Democrats championed the cause of women's suffrage and helped pass the Nineteenth Amendment, which was originally proposed by Roosevelt's Progressives.

Interest Groups

Interest groups play an important role in American government, influencing everything from elections to the policymaking process. Like political parties, interest groups can either be general or specifically dedicated to a single issue. An interest group may strongly favor a broad agenda, like fiscal conservatism, or pursue a single issue, such as healthcare. The stakeholders for interest groups range dramatically and can include foreign governments, corporations, or entire classes of people. Despite the differences between individual interest groups, they all share a common goal of amplifying the group's political power for valued issues. This is why most interest groups will lobby both major political parties, especially the party currently in power.

Similar to political parties' relationship to the electorate, interest groups can raise awareness and mobilize voters around their issues. For example, if an interest group believes a politician threatens their interest, they will fund and rally support for rival candidates. Interest groups have more access to officeholders than the average voter because they are among the largest campaign donors. Powerful interest groups even draft model legislation or model provisions for upcoming legislation, and it is not uncommon for the policymakers to include the interest group's language verbatim. This can sometimes be part of a healthy policymaking process, as when an interest group holds subject matter expertise in some obscure niche market. At the same time, interest groups can undermine representative government because they can exert pressure on politicians behind closed doors. Even if interest groups' influence is exaggerated, it creates the perception of corruption, especially when the public is unhappy with the current government.

Interest groups compete with professional organizations, social movements, and federal agencies during the critical stages of policymaking, such as the federal budget process or whenever Congress delegates authority to agencies. The federal budget process is particularly competitive because it involves the distribution of finite resources to fund the government's initiatives and programs. During this process, agencies and grassroots social movements lobby the government for funding, and interest groups lobby both the agencies and policymakers.

The Impact Relationships Have on Interest Groups' Influence

Aside from applying financial pressure, interest groups benefit from their longstanding relationship with bureaucratic agencies and congressional committees. The relationship between these three groups is sometimes called the "Iron Triangle" because the networks can last decades. Compared to elected representatives, bureaucrats can survive several unfavorable election cycles. Furthermore, the Iron Triangle includes a revolving door, allowing interest groups to enjoy even more access and control over government. Politicians and bureaucrats regularly leave the government and take positions in the private sector working for think tanks, corporations, or some other entity related to an interest group. Following this stint in the private sector, the former government official walks back through the revolving door and reenters the public sector. This revolving door creates the perception that government officials are favoring interest groups for personal gain, delegitimizing the government.

Factors that Affect the Influence of Interest Groups

Interest groups' financial control and longstanding relationships with public officials undermine democratic government. These groups are in a position to disproportionately influence policy, even overriding the base, because interest groups' campaign contributions carry such immense value under the current electoral system. Individual citizens can form interest groups to lobby candidates and the government, but they will need either money or massive support to compete at the same level of entrenched interest groups, such as corporations, trade associations, unions, and foreign powers. There's also a "free rider" problem where citizens think they can benefit from public interest groups without contributing time or money to the cause. For example, the constituency of working-class families is significantly greater than the constituency of investment banks. So, millions of working-class families will be free riders, depending on the other members of the constituency to fund and lead the interest group. In contrast, the constituency of investment bankers doesn't need to crowd source funding. The investment banks will gladly pay for everything because the more powerful the interest group, then the greater the opportunity for profit.

Single-Issue Political Groups

Single-issue groups, ideological and social movements, and protest movements generally operate with the goal of increasing awareness for their cause. As such, these groups and movements typically seek to influence powerful policymakers rather than attempt to personally succeed those policymakers. A notable exception is the Republican Party, which originated as a single-issue political party formed in opposition to the spread of slavery into the Western territories. The Green Party is more indicative of the usual single-issue group and movement.

Throughout its history, the **Green Party** has never posed a legitimate electoral challenge to the Democrats or Republicans but by advocating for a single-issue (environmental protection), it has influenced the major parties' platforms, especially the Democrats. Because there is more overlap between potential Democrat and Green Party voters, the Democrats have incentive to incorporate more environmental protection into their platform. The 2016 presidential election illustrates the risk of ignoring a popular single-issue party. In that election, Democratic presidential nominee, Hillary Clinton, paid insufficient attention to environmental issues. Her campaign posted some pro-environment policies on her campaign website, but environmental protection was rarely featured in her substantive campaign speeches. Consequently, the Democrats lost several key states by less than the margin of votes for the Green Party presidential candidate, Jill Stein.

An example of a protest movement that influenced society was the **anti-war movement**. Although both political establishments either ignored or outright despised the anti-war movement, the resulting increase to public awareness essentially forced the United States to withdraw from the Vietnam War. Similarly, the **Occupy Wall Street Movement** was an ideological movement that influenced society and politics without becoming a major political party. The Occupy Wall Street movement was an anti-capitalist reaction to the 2008 financial collapse that never received widespread support, but it directly laid the foundation for presidential candidates who were willing to criticize the "one percent" such as Bernie Sanders.

Civic Participation in a Representative Democracy

Factors that Affect the Process and Outcomes of Presidential Elections

Presidential elections draw significantly more interest from voters and media outlets than state or local elections. The presence of presidential elections broadens the political discussion because these candidates are often the election cycle's focal point from beginning to end. The presidency is by far the most powerful office an individual can hold due to the constitutional control presidents have over most of the federal bureaucracy.

Presidential candidates function as both symbolic figureheads and active leaders of their respective political party, and a popular presidential candidate can result in a "wave" election, meaning a single political party has a decisive advantage in all races. Among many factors, presidential elections are heavy influenced by down-ballot elections, a political party's primary system and nomination process, the incumbency advantage, and the Electoral College.

Down-ballot elections refers to congressional, state, and local elections that also take place during a presidential election cycle. These elections are called down-ballot races because presidential candidates appear at the top of voters' ballots, so every other race is literally further down on the ballot. The presidency is the election's headliner due to the greater political stakes related to the outcome. Increased access to fundraising and exposure strongly incentivize down-ballot candidates to follow the lead of their party's presidential candidate. At the same time, unpopular down-ballot candidates can harm the presidential candidate, but there's relatively less impact due to the presidential race's significantly higher profile.

Political parties generally field multiple presidential candidates, and they compete for their presidential nominations in primaries and caucuses held at the state level. Primaries can either be closed or open. **Closed primaries** mean that voters can vote only if they are a registered member of the political party, while **open primaries** are open to everyone. **Caucuses** are small meetings of voters, and the goal is to win the support of as many caucuses as possible.

When a candidate wins a state's primary or caucus, the victorious candidate receives that state's delegates to the party's nominating convention. The Democratic Party also sends super delegates to their convention, and these delegates are not bound to vote for any candidate. Conventions typically last for several days and feature speeches from the party's leadership. Following the convention, political parties' presidential candidates compete in the general election.

The **Electoral College** ultimately decides presidential elections. Under this system, every state is allotted a number of electoral votes, and a presidential candidate must win a majority of the electoral votes. If no candidate wins a majority of electoral votes, the election is decided in the House of Representatives.

States have the same number of electoral votes as congressional representatives. Electors cast electoral votes, and the electors are not technically legally bound to vote for the victorious candidate. However, no presidential election result has ever been overturned by electors changing their vote.

The Winner-Take-All System

Nearly all states use a winner-take-all-system to allocate their electoral votes with the two exceptions being Maine and Nebraska. As a result, the Electoral College is often criticized for being undemocratic because candidates sometimes win the popular vote and lose the election. In other words, the Electoral College essentially discounts the value of surplus votes because the margin of victory is irrelevant to the result in winner-take-all states. On the other hand, the Electoral College arguably upholds principles of representative government because it prevents the most populous states, such as New York and California, from dominating the election cycle, which would likely happen if the presidency were decided by popular vote.

Sitting presidents typically enjoy an incumbency advantage. Although all major party candidates enjoy enormous influence during presidential elections, sitting presidents have a larger public platform. When the president chooses to speak on a hot button issue, it is almost always major news, which amounts to free publicity for the president's reelection campaign. As such, the incumbency advantage phenomenon can be attributed to the office's high profile. Prior to the 2016 election, the last three presidents—Barack Obama, George W. Bush, and Bill Clinton—all won reelection and served two terms.

Factors that Affect the Process and Outcomes of Congressional Elections

Congressional elections occur every two years; they either run concurrently with presidential elections, or if there is no presidential election, congressional elections are referred to as mid-term elections. All seats in the House of Representatives are contested during congressional elections. In contrast, 33 or 34 of the 100 Senate seats are contested because U.S. Senators serve for a term of six years, and the terms are staggered every 2 years.

Congressional elections feature the same state-held caucuses and primaries as presidential elections. The primary difference between the presidential and congressional nomination and election processes is the scale. Presidential elections attract more money and attention from constituents, party leaders, and the voting public. As such, the barrier for entry is lower because less money is required to attempt a primary challenge or run a congressional campaign, though congressional elections have dramatically increased in cost over recent years.

Congressional candidates have increasingly come to rely on their presidential candidates because successful presidential campaigns can carry down-ballot candidates to victory. This is especially true if the presidential candidate is more popular than the local candidate within their district. Presidential candidates are also more likely to draw nonvoters to the ballot box, and these voters are more likely to vote for other candidates from the same party because they agree with the presidential candidate.

Generally speaking, congressional incumbents are heavy favorites over primary challengers as well as in the general election. Congressional incumbents usually have larger public profiles and name recognition within their districts as compared to their opponents. In addition, congressional incumbents have already won an election and wielded power for at least one term, so they typically have an advantage in fundraising due to their preexisting donor network and campaign infrastructure.

Despite these advantages, congressional incumbents occasionally lose in primaries. This is most often the case when the incumbent has lost their connection to the base. For example, Tea Party activists stunned the Republican Party after winning primary challenges against established congressional leaders. Republican House leader Eric Cantor lost a primary race in 2014, and at that time, his defeat was considered one of the most surprising results in modern American political history. One year later, Republican right-wing representatives ousted their fellow Republican, John Boehner, from his role of Majority Speaker of the House in another shocking move. Boehner likely would have met the same fate as Cantor in a primary contest, which explains why he immediately resigned from the House of Representatives altogether. Cantor and Boehner had defied the base by supporting a bipartisan immigration agreement, which was a divisive issue within the Republican Party before becoming a national issue during the 2016 presidential election. This illustrates how primary contests shape political parties' relationship to base and governing strategy.

Modern Political Campaigns

Political campaigns have experienced a massive shift over recent years. Compared to earlier eras, modern campaigns last much longer, cost significantly more money, depend on political consultants, and incorporate cutting-edge innovations in communication technology.

The rising demand and increasing supply of around-the-clock political coverage and analysis has significantly extended the campaign season. Previously, a candidate would only need to spend several months campaigning for their party's nomination and then several more months campaigning during the general election. In the present day, candidates spend months preparing for a primary or general election campaign, and those campaigns are longer than ever before. There is considerable advantage to being the first candidate to enter the race, such as maximizing the amount of time spent rallying grassroots support and raising money. As a result, it is not uncommon for candidates to announce "exploratory campaigns" more than a year before any ballots are cast.

Modern political campaigns extensively rely on professional consultants. Technological innovation has forced politicians to conduct messaging on new platforms, like social media, and it has created opportunities for candidates to leverage the massive amount of data available for every voter. Social media offers a unique opportunity for campaigns because it is both an effective way to crowd fund campaign contributions from supporters and instantaneously disseminate messaging to millions of people. In regard to data, professional consultants can harness the skill and expertise of specialists to tailor messaging directly to the voters' values or priorities.

Nearly every national candidate spends a significant amount of money on consultants, and political parties retain consultants to advise on broader strategy and messaging. However, relying on consultants can sometimes work to representatives' detriment. Consultants often have other clients and preexisting relationships, and due to the money involved, these clients are typically of a powerful interest group. Even if the consultant is free of such conflicts, using consultants can make candidates appear less genuine and relatable.

Election cycles have increased in duration for a variety of reasons. For one, there has been rising demand for political news, largely due to cable news and the Internet's ability to deliver content around the clock. While the percentage of citizens who vote has remained relatively low, the segment of citizens who are interested in politics has become more passionate, consuming political media on a daily basis from multiple sources. Another major reason is the push from states to move primary contests earlier and earlier. The Iowa caucus has been the first primary election since the 1972 election cycle, and whenever other states have attempted to become the first primary election, the Iowa caucus has also been moved up. States are interested in holding primary and caucus earlier in the campaign season because candidates begin campaigning in those states' months before any other state. This attracts media attention and raises the profile of those states' local issues, like Iowa and New Hampshire, prior to the actual start of the campaign season.

Along with the reliance on professional consultants and broader messaging strategies, longer campaigns have directly contributed to the exponential explosion in the cost of political campaigns. For example, $1.6 billion was spent during the entire 1998 mid-term election cycle, and $5.7 billion was spent during the 2018 mid-term election cycle. Consequently, political parties and campaigns have increased their fundraising efforts, particularly after recent changes to campaign finance law.

Campaign Finance Law

Campaign finance law has been weakened since the 1970s. In *Buckley v. Valeo* (1976), the Supreme Court of the United States upheld the **Federal Election Campaign Act's** (1971) limits on contributions for individual citizens and requirements for disclosure of campaign contributions due to states' interest in running less corrupt elections. However, the Court overturned limits on how much money a campaign could spend on an election, rules for independent expenditures, and candidates financing their own campaigns.

The Bipartisan Campaign Reform Act of 2002
The **Bipartisan Campaign Reform Act of 2002 (BCRA)**, also known as the **McCain-Feingold Act**, attempted to address issues in campaign finance law. The Act imposed restrictions on electioneering communications and using "soft money," meaning alternative sources of financing to standard contributions made to political parties. In addition, BCRA attempted to increase accountability by forcing candidates to say, "I'm Politician X and I approve this message." However, BCRA did not address the rising problem of nonprofits exploiting legal loopholes to attack presidential and congressional candidates. For example, wealthy conservatives funded a nonprofit, Swift Vets and POWs for Truth, to launch baseless character assassinations against Democratic presidential candidate John Kerry during the 2004 election.

Citizens United v. Federal Election Commission
Campaign finance laws were further loosened by the Supreme Court's decision in *Citizens United v. Federal Election Commission* (2010). The Court decided to permit organizations to use corporate and union money for electioneering communications, and it lifted limits on contributions to political organizations as long as the organization did not officially "coordinate" with the campaign. In effect, *Citizens United* allows for individuals, corporations, unions, and entities to spend unlimited money on elections through **Super PACs (Political Action Committees),** which will be discussed in greater detail shortly.

Debates Over Free Speech and Campaign Funding

The Supreme Court has based its decision to overturn campaign finance restrictions on the need to protect citizens' free speech rights under the First Amendment. The Court has equated money with speech because citizens can use money to buy advertisements and otherwise communicate with their fellow voters. While equating money with speech makes logical sense, the resulting increase to big money donor's influence on elections has been controversial. Critics of *Citizens United* argue it legalizes corruption because it is a quid pro quo agreement between politicians and powerful interest groups. Politicians depend on contributions from Super PACs, so it would be expected that politicians would favor big money donors to receive their continued support. There continues to be a debate over how free speech protections and concerns over corruption should be balanced, especially as income inequality continues to increase.

Types of Political Action Committees (PACs)

Rather than standard PACs, which still have contribution limits, Super PACs have almost no restrictions as long as they act "independently." While Super PACs don't officially coordinate with campaigns on a strictly legal basis, they are de facto part of a candidate's campaign strategy, particularly in fundraising efforts. Because individual and legal entities' contributions to campaigns and PACs are capped, Super PACs allow candidates to raise massive amounts of funds from big money donors. In addition, Super PACs are led by people with preexisting relationships with the candidate and their campaign. As such, the independence of Super PACs is a legal fiction as a practical matter.

Modern Media Environment

Technological innovation has forever altered how citizens acquire information about current events and the political climate. Cable television first fractured the media environment through the creation of 24/7 networks solely dedicated to the news. Prior to the 1980s, most Americans received political news from the same broadcast news programs, a handful of national newspapers and magazines, and local news outlets, collectively referred to as **traditional media**.

The Cable News Network (CNN) was established in 1980, becoming the first 24/7 cable news channel, and Fox News and MSNBC both debuted in 1996. These three cable news channels still constitute some of the most influential platforms within the media. In addition, the *New York Times, Wall Street Journal*, and *Washington Post* are all daily newspapers with national audiences, and there are several national magazines that have retained significant readerships, such as *The Atlantic, The Economist, The New Yorker*, and *Time*. However, the rise of the Internet during the early twentieth century dramatically disrupted the news industry. Now, all of these traditional media outlets host content on digital platforms, and they must compete with online publications, blogs, and social media.

The new media environment has fundamentally changed the relationship between citizens and news coverage. When traditional media dominated the industry, citizens were passive consumers of news. The traditional media dictated what was covered and how it was covered, and there was a limited supply of alternative perspectives. Following the creation of the digital landscape, consumers can now follow current events in real time, particularly on social media. For example, citizens can follow election results in real time, as votes are being counted, rather than waiting for a cable network or newspaper to provide the final results.

The explosion of digital outlets has also led to the creation of nearly unlimited market niches, so citizens can obtain information about seemingly any topic at any time. More outlets than ever are also conducting investigative journalism. Investigative journalists spend a significant amount of time on a specific topic, such as political scandals, and they deliver a detailed report that's similar to what a law enforcement department would produce. Despite the many advantages of empowering citizens to be active consumers of news, there are significant dangers in this new media landscape.

Issues in Media

Fierce competition between media outlets has resulted in market niches where outlets cater to specific ideological preferences. Fox News is the most commonly cited example of this trend. Since its inception, the Murdoch family, which owns Fox News as well as several other media companies, has been vocal about its desire to counter what they perceive as liberal bias in other mainstream media. As such, the network offers news coverage from a conservative perspective. Tailoring coverage to people's preferences has driven viewership and churned massive profits. Fox News currently dwarfs its cable news competitors, MSNBC and CNN, in terms of viewership. In response to Fox News capturing nearly the entire conservative audience, MSNBC and CNN have drifted more toward the liberal perspective. However, media outlets with a liberal bias are more concerned with hearing from "both sides." For example, criticism of the Republican Party is increasingly rare on Fox News, while MSNBC and CNN routinely critique the Democratic Party in terms of strategy and execution.

Although Fox News, MSNBC, and CNN hold different ideological perspectives, they each engage in similar practices that skew coverage. All three networks are also owned by large multinational corporate entities. As such, any criticism of capitalism is exceedingly rare if not nonexistent. Instead, socialists are characterized as people with liberal positions in "culture wars" and "identity politics," which are both incredibly difficult to define. In contrast, fringe libertarian positions that poll less favorably than socialism—like eliminating the inheritance tax or dismantling much of the government—are discussed as if they are serious policy proposals. This is unsurprising when considering the financial incentives at play. Corporate ownership and decision makers belong to a different economic class than their audience, and they stand to benefit from characterizing anything with the appearance of "socialism" as nothing more than fringe extremism.

Furthermore, ownership groups often have high-stake legal matters before the government. For example, CNN is currently owned by AT&T, which is undergoing a multibillion-dollar corporate merger that requires the Trump administration's approval. Conservatives have criticized CNN for their negative coverage of the Trump campaign and presidency. Even if the pending corporate merger has not motivated CNN's negative coverage, it inarguably creates a perception of a conflict of interest.

Along with the country's national newspapers, the three cable news networks all rarely criticize the United States' interventionist foreign policy. The most infamous example of this phenomenon was the runup to the Iraq War where nearly all political outlets published the George W. Bush administration's version of events with minimal pushback. The fallout of this coverage directly contributed to plummeting trust in media, particularly because it was not an isolated incident. American media outlets regularly discuss the necessity of military intervention to uphold America's commitment to human rights.

At the same time, these same outlets rarely mention the possibility of intervention deepening those very same human rights crises. For example, nearly every mainstream media outlet is covering the ongoing humanitarian crisis in Venezuela without mentioning the possible backlash to any attempt at intervention. The amount of coverage dedicated to Venezuela is exponentially greater than the coverage of the situation in Yemen where the United States is actively partnering with Saudi Arabia to inflict a comparable humanitarian crisis on one of the poorest countries in the world. Such startling discrepancies raise serious questions about the mainstream media's ability to provide "unbiased" news coverage.

Aside from media ownership, there is also significant bias in how all mainstream media outlets select and analyze news stories. Most media outlets follow the rule of thumb "if it bleeds, it leads" to guide the selection and priority of stories. In effect, media outlets provide sensational coverage of "breaking" news stories that feature violence to the detriment of systemic issues. Media outlets often dedicate 24/7 coverage to mass shooting events as they occur in real time, and then the coverage disappears until the next mass shooting occurs. Skewing coverage toward breaking news buries long-term trends that have just as serious consequences for the country. For example, the opioid crisis kills approximately 50,000 Americans per year, and it receives less coverage on mainstream media than political scandals that involve sexual impropriety.

Another source of bias is that news outlets have increasingly hired political commentators rather than journalists. This has resulted in a rise in opinions masquerading as journalism with the most obvious being cable news segments with political commentators screaming talking points at each other. Media outlets are largely motivated by the pursuit of profit as expressed in viewership. The average person prefers to be entertained rather than informed, so media outlets often prioritizes entertainment over substantive and informative content, especially when their viewership is likely to disagree with the subject matter.

Hiring more political commentators and allowing media consumers to dictate coverage has led to mainstream media outlets turning politics into a series of "horse races." Media coverage often focuses on political candidates' charisma and relative popularity as opposed to qualifications or meaningful distinctions in their platforms. The mainstream media also overwhelmingly focuses on the short term. As a result, daily coverage emphasizes whether candidates won or lost in the polls that day. This is particularly ineffective because polling is an imperfect science. Polls provide probability based on a specific cross-segment of the population, and they can be skewed based on how the questions are phrased.

Additionally, political horse races turn political commentators into prognostications, and it undermines their credibility when their predictions are incorrect. The 2016 presidential election proved particularly embarrassing for mainstream media's horse race coverage. Every mainstream media platform, including conservative outlets like Fox News and the Wall Street Journal, mocked the launch of Trump's campaign. It was covered as a spectacle for the express purpose of entertaining viewers. Once Trump won the Republican nomination, the mainstream media firmly labeled him as a massive underdog. As Election Day approached, various polls pegged Trump's chances of winning between five and forty percent. Political commentators should have told their audiences that a Clinton victory was probable and a Trump victory was possible. Instead, countless "expert" political commentators vocally announced the election was effectively over before votes were cast. The American voters proved the media wrong, adding to the growing lack of trust in mainstream media coverage.

Media's Impact on Political Landscape

Media plays an essential role in disseminating information to the public, and representative government requires an informed public that's willing and able to participate politically, such as engaging in democratic debate. Social media has increasingly turned into a public forum, and conversations have increasingly turned political, even when the subject of debate isn't inherently political, like movies or sports. Due to the increased media coverage, citizens are now consuming more political content than ever before. However, if the public consumes misleading or sensational political coverage, political participation will become more explosive, undermining the state of democratic debate. Several factors within the media environment influence whether the citizenry is informed enough to contribute toward a healthy democratic debate, including the proliferation of media choices, ideological programming, technological innovation, and credibility issues.

The proliferation of media choices is a double-edged sword. On the one hand, the government and powerful private actors have more difficulty controlling the narrative. Prior to cable television and the

Internet, there were only a handful of news programs and national newspapers. If those programs and newspapers were compromised, then the public could more easily be misled. In the present-day, media outlets frequently challenge their competitors' reporting and analysis. As such, citizens have the opportunity to consume multiple sides of the same story and draw their own conclusions.

On the other hand, the proliferation of media choices allows citizens to pick and choose what they consume. If a citizen reads the same news story in ten sources holding the same ideological perspective, they're more likely to believe the story is true and regard contradictory stories as "fake news." Ideological programming and technological information have contributed to this growing phenomenon of personalized news coverage. Some media outlets even intentionally tailor content to their audiences' ideology, and technological innovation allows citizens to cultivate their own personal news feed, such as what's occurred on social media. Credibility issues further entrench people in their beliefs, especially when a news outlet is seemingly incapable of criticizing a specific political party or candidate. The cumulative result of these trends is an American public that's increasingly ideological, arrogant, and unwilling to engage in democratic debate with people holding different views.

Practice Questions

1. Compared to PACs, what makes Super PACs unique?

    a. PACs have campaign contribution limits, while Super PACs do not, as long as the Super PAC doesn't coordinate with the campaign.

    b. Super PACs are able to receive financial contributions from prospective voters, while PACs cannot.

    c. PACs are always led by congressional leaders, while Super PACs only need to operate independently from political campaigns.

    d. Super PACs are classified as for-profit businesses, while PACs are classified as nonprofit organizations.

Question 2 refers to the following table:

Electoral College Results (2000)		
Party	Popular Votes	Electoral Votes
Constitution	98,020	0
Democratic	50,999,897	266
Green	2,882,955	0
Libertarian	384,431	0
Natural Law	83,714	0
Reform	448,895	0
Republican	50,456,002	271
Other	51,186	0
Abstention	n/a	1

2. Which party's candidate won the 2000 presidential election?

    a. Democratic

    b. Green

    c. Libertarian

    d. Republican

3. Joel is a prospective voter in the upcoming presidential general election. He has never voted in an election before, but Joel has been inspired by the Green Party's presidential candidate. Joel is particularly impressed by how the presidential candidate is leading the party in a new direction with a broad policy agenda. Given these circumstances, which of the following statements is most likely TRUE?

    a. Joel is more likely to be a party-line voter than a rational-choice voter.

    b. Joel is more likely to be a retrospective voter than a prospective voter.

    c. Joel is more likely to be a single-issue voter than a rational-choice voter.

    d. Joel is more likely to be a nonvoter than a voter.

Questions 4–5 refer to the following passage:

All obstructions to the execution of the laws, all combinations and associations, under whatever plausible character, with the real design to direct, control, counteract, or awe the regular deliberation and action of the constituted authorities, are destructive of this fundamental principle, and of fatal tendency...

However combinations or associations of the above description may now and then answer popular ends, they are likely, in the course of time and things, to become potent engines, by which cunning, ambitious, and unprincipled men will be enabled to subvert the power of the people and to usurp for themselves the reins of government, destroying afterwards the very engines which have lifted them to unjust dominion.

- George Washington, *Farewell Address* (1796)

4. According to George Washington, what is the problem with combinations and associations?
   a. Combinations and associations are strictly prohibited by the U.S. Constitution.
   b. Combinations and associations compete with political parties' dominance over the electoral system.
   c. Combinations and associations destroy political parties and replace them with unprincipled oligarchs.
   d. Combinations and associations lead to the consolidation of political power and increased corruption.

5. How would George Washington most likely react to the state of modern political parties?
   a. George Washington would support the two-party system because a third major party would lead to more factionalism.
   b. George Washington would be concerned over modern political parties' fundraising capacity and influence over government.
   c. George Washington would support the trend toward more candidate-centered campaigns.
   d. George Washington would encourage grassroots activists to seize control over modern political parties' infrastructure.

6. What does the Iron Triangle refer to?
   a. The Iron Triangle refers to a campaign strategy deployed by political parties to win the support of the working class.
   b. The Iron Triangle refers to the influence of corporations on tariffs and free trade deals.
   c. The Iron Triangle refers to an economic policy intended to boost the American manufacturing sector.
   d. The Iron Triangle refers to the enduring relationship shared by bureaucratic agencies, congressional committees, and interest groups.

7. The Purple Political Party (PPP) has become one of the two major political parties in the United States. In addition, compared to all other political parties, the PPP has by far the strongest linkage institutions. In recent years, however, various political controversies have led to the disclosure of several conflicts of interest within the PPP's campaign infrastructure and consultants. Which of the following statements is MOST likely to be true about the PPP as described in this fact pattern?

    a. The PPP will gain more grassroots support because strong linkage institutions can better support more extensive campaign infrastructure.

    b. The PPP will increase in popularity because the controversy will lead to more media coverage.

    c. The PPP is at risk of losing its frontrunner status because the conflicts of interest with interest groups could create a perception of corruption.

    d. The PPP will remain the leading major political party because it still has the strongest linkage institutions.

Question 8 refers to the following passage:

Voter enthusiasm plummeted yesterday immediately after the news spread about unprecedented wait times at the polls. Many local residents, like social media star Jonathan Hastings, claimed to have seen lines stretching more than four city blocks at South Islip High School. As the polls closed late last night, government watchdog groups vowed to investigate whether the state failed to provide adequate resources to the local election board, and if so, whether it was an intentional act of sabotage.

- Wallace David, *South Islip Gazette*, Nov. 4, 2020

8. What voter demographic was the most likely to have been disproportionately harmed by the unprecedented wait times?

    a. White voters

    b. Working class voters

    c. Older voters

    d. Male voters

Question 9 refers to the following diagram:

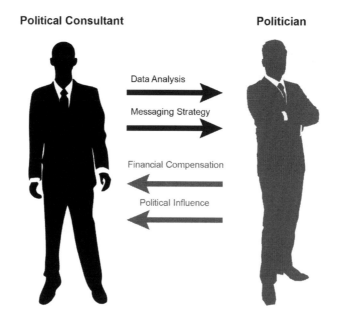

G30

9. Which of the following statements BEST describes how the Politician benefits from the relationship depicted above?

    a. The politician will likely be able to spend less money during their less election cycle.

    b. The politician will likely enhance the effectiveness of their campaign communication through tailored advertisements.

    c. The politician will likely increase their popularity by appearing more genuine and relatable to voters.

    d. The politician will be able to better analyze economic data to develop policies that benefit an increased number of constituents.

10. How does the Fifteenth Amendment compare to the Seventeenth Amendment in regard to the expansion of democracy in the United States?

    a. The Fifteenth Amendment increased the number of eligible voters, and the Seventeenth Amendment established the popular election of U.S. Senators.

    b. The Fifteenth Amendment guaranteed the right to vote for people regardless of sex, and the Seventeenth Amendment established the popular election of U.S. Senators.

    c. The Fifteenth Amendment prohibited discrimination based on race, and the Seventeenth Amendment limited political corruption by prohibiting the sale of alcohol.

    d. The Fifteenth Amendment lowered the eligible voting age, and the Seventeenth Amendment created the Electoral College.

11. Why did the Bipartisan Campaign Reform Act of 2002 ultimately fail to achieve its goals?

    a. The Supreme Court ruled the entire Act was unconstitutional due to free speech violations.

    b. The Supreme Court struck down the Act's key provisions in its landmark case *Buckley v. Valeo*.

    c. The Act allowed nonprofit organizations to continue attacking political candidates.

    d. The Act failed to impose restrictions on electioneering communications.

12. How do congressional election cycles compare to presidential election cycles?
    a. Congressional election cycles are typically longer.
    b. Congressional election cycles receive more campaign contributions.
    c. Presidential election cycles attract more media attention.
    d. Presidential election cycles are easier for third-party candidates to win.

Answer Explanations

1. A: Standard political action committees (PACs) coordinate their fundraising and messaging efforts with political candidates, so they are subject to campaign contribution limits. In contrast, the Supreme Court eliminated restrictions on campaign contributions to political action committees that don't officially coordinate with campaigns, and these are called Super PACs. Thus, Choice *A* is correct. Choice *B* is incorrect because both PACs and Super PACs can receive financial contributions from prospective voters. PACs are not always led by congressional leaders. Because PACs coordinate with political campaigns, candidates are typically involved in choosing their PACs' leadership. So, Choice *C* is incorrect. Choice *D* is incorrect because Super PACs are also classified as nonprofit organizations.

2. D: The Electoral College is how presidential elections are decided in the United States. Presidential candidates must win a majority of electoral votes to win the election. The table shows that the Republican candidate won 271 electoral votes, which constitutes a majority of the total electoral votes. Thus, Choice *D* is correct. Although the Democratic candidate won the popular vote, the Electoral College only counts electoral votes; therefore, Choice *A* is incorrect. Choices *B* and *C* are both incorrect because neither party's candidate won a single electoral vote.

3. A: Joel has been inspired to vote based on the Green Party's presidential candidate. In addition, he supports the presidential candidate's influence on the Green Party. Because Joel is a nonvoter, it's likely he doesn't particularly support any other political party. So, Joel will likely be a party-line voter. He believes in the Green Party candidate's vision, and even if he doesn't particularly support other Green Party candidates, he will likely vote for them to support the presidential candidate. Thus, Choice *A* is correct. Choice *B* is incorrect because the prompt doesn't mention Joel's opinion on politicians' past performance, so he's unlikely to be a retrospective voter. Choice *C* is incorrect because Joel supports the presidential candidate's broad policy agenda, so he likely isn't a single-issue voter. Choice *D* is incorrect because Joel has been inspired by a presidential candidate whom he plans to support.

4. D: George Washington is criticizing combinations and associations for directing, controlling, counteracting, and aweing the constituted authorities (government). As a result, he believes this consolidation of political power will lead to unprincipled men seizing control to further their self-interest, causing a rise in corruption. Thus, Choice *D* is correct. Choice *A* is incorrect because George Washington never mentions the U.S. Constitution or argues that combinations and associations are unconstitutional. Choices *B* and *C* are both incorrect because political parties are combinations and associations, which George Washington doesn't support.

5. B: Modern political parties operate like corporations. Major parties can raise billions of dollars in a relatively short period of time, and they have thousands of employees and volunteers who are organized in a complex bureaucracy. Modern political parties function as powerful combinations and associations, which George Washington doesn't support. Thus, Choice *B* is correct. George Washington would not support consolidating political power into two parties, so Choice *A* is incorrect. Choice *C* is incorrect because George Washington doesn't mention candidate-centered campaigns. Although George Washington would support grassroots activists running the government more than powerful political parties, his preference would be for political parties not to exist. So, Choice *D* is incorrect.

6. D: The Iron Triangle refers to the relationship between bureaucratic agencies, congressional committees, and interest groups. The relationship is enduring because the networks can last decades. Thus, Choice *D* is correct. Choice *A* does not describe a relationship between three entities, so it is incorrect. Choice B is incorrect because Iron Triangle doesn't refer to corporate influence on tariffs and free trade deals, though some individual corporations do leverage the Iron Triangle to achieve those goals. Likewise, the Iron Triangle doesn't refer to implementing economic policy, so Choice C is incorrect.

7. C: Linkage institutions are channels of communication between representatives, political staff, and constituents. Theoretically, strong linkage institutions will result in electoral success, but the linkage institutions can be undermined if the party loses grassroots support. Controversies over conflicts of interest or overreliance on consultants can result in a loss of grassroots support. Thus, Choice C is correct. Strong linkage institutions can support large campaign infrastructure, but the PPP is more likely to struggle with grassroots support due to the conflicts of interest, so Choice A is incorrect. It is unclear why negative media coverage over an ongoing controversy would make the PPP more popular, so Choice B is incorrect. The PPP will likely remain a major political party due to its strong linkage institutions, but it might not be the leading party due to the controversy. So, Choice D is incorrect.

8. B: The unprecedented delays would pose the greatest issue to citizens who cannot afford to wait. Logistical problems with elections pose a structural barrier to working class voters because hourly workers typically have less flexibility to miss time at work. Thus, Choice B is correct. White voters, older voters, and male voters would all be inconvenienced by the delays, but they would not disproportionately harmed in the same way as working-class voters. So, Choices A, C, and D are all incorrect.

9. B: The diagram illustrates a politician's relationship with a political consultant. The politician is paying money and providing access to power in exchange for assistance with data analytics and messaging strategy. As such, the politician would likely be using the political consultant's expertise in those areas for the purpose of tailoring advertisements to voters' values and priorities. Thus, Choice B is correct. The politician is paying the political consultant, and there's no evidence that this relationship will save the politician money during the election cycle, so Choice A is incorrect. Data analysis and messaging strategy is more closely related to political advertising than increasing a candidate's personal popularity, so Choice C is incorrect. Choice D is incorrect because the diagram doesn't reference a populist economic program.

10. A: The Fifteenth Amendment expanded democracy by prohibiting the denial of voting rights based on "race, color, or previous condition of servitude," which increased the number of eligible voters. The Seventeenth Amendment expanded democracy by establishing the popular election of U.S. Senators. Thus, Choice A is correct. Choice B is incorrect because the Nineteenth Amendment guaranteed the right to vote for people regardless of sex. Choice C is incorrect because the Fourteenth Amendment prohibited discrimination based on race, and the Eighteenth Amendment prohibited the sale of alcohol. Choice D is incorrect because the Twenty-Sixth Amendment lowered the eligible voting age, and the Twelfth Amendment reformed the Electoral College.

11. C: The Bipartisan Campaign Reform Act of 2002 sought to address abuses in campaign finance law. The Act did impose restrictions on soft money and electioneering, but it failed to achieve its goal because the Act didn't stop nonprofit organizations from attacking political candidates. Choice A alludes to the Supreme Court's decision in *Citizens United*, but that case didn't overturn the entire Act. So, Choice A is incorrect. Choice B is incorrect because the Supreme Court decided *Buckley* in 1976, so that case preceded the Act by several decades. The Act did impose restrictions on electioneering communications; therefore, Choice D is incorrect.

12. C: Presidential election cycles dwarf congressional elections in terms of coverage. Although the executive and legislative branches are coequal, the presidency is a much more powerful position than any individual congressional office. Because there is more voter interest in presidential races and higher profile candidates run for president, there is significantly more media coverage. Thus, Choice *C* is correct. Presidential election cycles occur every four years, and congressional elections take place every two years. So, Choice *A* is incorrect because it states the opposite. Choice *B* is incorrect because presidential elections are more costly than congressional elections. Choice *D* is incorrect because a third-party candidate has never won a presidential election.

Dear AP U.S. Government & Politics Exam Taker,

We would like to start by thanking you for purchasing this study guide for your exam. We hope that we exceeded your expectations.

Our goal in creating this study guide was to cover all of the topics that you will see on the test. We also strove to make our practice questions as similar as possible to what you will encounter on test day. With that being said, if you found something that you feel was not up to your standards, please send us an email and let us know.

We would also like to let you know about other books in our catalog that may interest you.

AP Comparative Government and Politics	amazon.com/dp/1628456167
AP Biology	amazon.com/dp/1628456221
SAT	amazon.com/dp/1628456396
ACT	amazon.com/dp/162845606X

We have study guides in a wide variety of fields. If the one you are looking for isn't listed above, then try searching for it on Amazon or send us an email.

Thanks Again and Happy Testing!
Product Development Team
info@studyguideteam.com

Interested in buying more than 10 copies of our product? Contact us about bulk discounts:

bulkorders@studyguideteam.com

FREE Test Taking Tips DVD Offer

To help us better serve you, we have developed a Test Taking Tips DVD that we would like to give you for FREE. **This DVD covers world-class test taking tips that you can use to be even more successful when you are taking your test.**

All that we ask is that you email us your feedback about your study guide. Please let us know what you thought about it – whether that is good, bad or indifferent.

To get your **FREE Test Taking Tips DVD**, email freedvd@studyguideteam.com with "FREE DVD" in the subject line and the following information in the body of the email:

    a. The title of your study guide.

    b. Your product rating on a scale of 1-5, with 5 being the highest rating.

    c. Your feedback about the study guide. What did you think of it?

    d. Your full name and shipping address to send your free DVD.

If you have any questions or concerns, please don't hesitate to contact us at freedvd@studyguideteam.com.

Thanks again!

61525903R00067

Made in the USA
Columbia, SC
23 June 2019